1991

Managing IT at Board Level

THE HIDDEN AGENDA EXPOSED

Managing IT at Board Level

THE HIDDEN AGENDA EXPOSED

Kit Grindley

Professor of Systems Automation at the London School of Economics, Price Waterhouse Consultant

Pitman

Pitman Publishing
128 Long Acre, London WC2E 9AN

A Division of Longman Group UK Limited

First published in 1991

© Price Waterhouse 1991

British Library Cataloguing in Publication Data
Grindley, Kit
 Managing IT at board level: Exposing the hidden
 agenda.
 I. Title
 658.400285

ISBN 0 273 03455 3

Typeset by Falcon Typographic Art Ltd, Edinburgh
Printed and bound in Great Britain

Contents

Note: The title of the computer department, and of the executives who run them, varies from country to country, and fashionably, from time to time. For the sake of consistency, we have adopted the terms IT department, IT executives and IT director throughout the text.

Preface

It seems that IT is at a crossroads. Conscious that we are entering a computer controlled world, chief executives are busy appointing IT directors to sort it all out. These newcomers to the board are perfectly aware that computers no longer have to be run by large centralized data processing departments, however. They could gain some easy popularity by following today's business fashion to decentralize everything in sight, and let the users do their own thing with their own computers.

The problem with this is infrastructure. The management of IT at Board level is either the short-term role of taking the mystique out of computing, and managing the difficult task of splitting up the existing centralized IT department by distributing its function amongst the users; or the long-term role of building communications infrastructures, information storage infrastructures and data capture and data processing infrastructures, to support and integrate the do-it-yourself user movement.

The investigations which have lead to this book convince me that the first of these routes is the more popular. What more natural a reaction to the over-centralization of the past? By the turn of the century, however, we will probably be complaining of over-decentralization, and be embarking on the even more difficult task of clawing back what we will then be able to identify as the key components of the organization's central nervous system.

Kit Grindley
The London School of Economics
September, 1991

Acknowledgements

This book is based entirely on opinions given by the five thousand IT executives who are members of the Price Waterhouse international Computer Opinion Panel, and of a further research programme, conducted in 102 major corporations throughout the world who have appointed IT directors.

Thanks are due:

to Price Waterhouse, for making the survey information available, and for sponsoring the special research project

to the editorial panel of Price Waterhouse partners, who guided both the research, and the analysis of the findings

Tony Havlin
Clive Newton
Bob Pamplin
Roger Pavitt
Noel Taylor

and, principally, to the IT executives who gave so freely of their time, their opinions and their experience.

Whilst the book is entirely the product of a Price Waterhouse Management Consultancy initiative, the opinions expressed, and the experiences related, are those of the IT executives interviewed.

Part 1

INTRODUCTION

‘‘What did we think it was?’
　　‘Some say a giant brain’
‘Did it think for us?’
　　‘Others say a replacement for people’
‘What sort of people did it replace?’
　　‘Those that followed rules’
‘Well then, there you have it – it’s a rule-following machine’
　　‘But who wants a rule-following machine?’’’

Chapter 1

Enthusiasts versus pragmatists

❝ We control the computer. After all, we write the programs. But, once they're up and running, we seem to lose the control we thought we had **❞**

There was a well-known guru going the rounds in the sixties. His favourite stories were about programmers: how they failed to meet deadlines, cut their hair, document their work, dry run their programs before testing, and wear shoes. He got a lot of laughs. He hated programmers. So did we. He taught that they could be controlled; some basic work measurement, he said, set performance standards and insist on feedback that you can touch, not just 'say so' and promises.

We liked that message. It was so obviously right. It was the basic management technique for planning and controlling every other workforce; it had worked for Taylor, Gilbreth and Bedaux forty years before; it had worked for all of us ever since. And, after all, what was so special about developing computer systems?

So, back at the office, we tried out what the guru had said. And here we are, thirty years on, with the year 2000 just around the corner. And most of us still haven't met a deadline. Especially if you include 'to cost' and 'to quality'. But 'how do you measure program quality?' you're saying. Oh, dear! And the book's hardly started.

The guru also reminded us that programmers arrived at work around ten or eleven in the morning. And then read the paper. He acknowledged they could read. What he failed to mention was that, in those days, they didn't leave at five o'clock – or six, or eight, or, occasionally, until midnight. Sometimes they worked all night.

The guru said that their salaries were more than the chief executive's in some cases. And most of them had only just left school.

We couldn't laugh any more. Our breath had gone; the pain was intense. And the truth hurt too. What made it worse, a sixteen year old programmer had been reported in the press that week, saying 'I don't know why they pay me for this job. I write programs at home for a hobby.'

The history of computing seems unique from this point of view. It seems to polarize the two basic attitudes to progress: the enthusiasts, who love every nut and bolt, cherish the machine's imperfections, but hold unswervingly to the construction of an ideal version that will save the world; and the pragmatists, who are unconcerned how things work, desire only to learn the controls, and assess each invention solely by its practical bearing upon human interests.

This would be of only academic importance, if it were not for the size of the world investment in computers which has taken place in the last four decades of this century. And if it were not so conspicuously the case that, for the first three decades at least, this investment was driven by the enthusiasts, and that today, the chief executives of the world's largest companies state frankly that they cannot measure value for money from this investment.

In a nutshell, that is what this book is about. How can we exert bottom line control over runaway IT enthusiasm?

What has been astonishing to many is how people can get so enthusiastic about computers. They do not look particularly beautiful. Most of the world's largest installations have the glamour of a white goods discount store with no price tickets. The only excitement for a visitor is getting through the massive security precautions which surround them.

And they don't do anything, these stationary boxes. The small ones are provided with keyboards, and demand the users acquire some typing skills; something we made our daughters promise they wouldn't learn. And their screens flicker messages back, in a way which concerns the health watchdogs in many of our trade unions, and understandably so.

But there it is. Millions are turned on by the challenge of programming these machines. And millions more are excited by the possibility of automation, to the point of creating artificial intelligence.

Let's be clear: some hard-nosed managers are not immune to the computer's charms.

Case

A veteran computer consultant reported his experience of the early days of the computer's invasion of business. 'I had an important client in the manufacturing sector. We were undertaking a computer justification study – these studies must have been the most popular use of consultants in those days. Manufacturing businesses were difficult cases. They weren't like the financial institutions or the public utilities, where you had one, basic, high data volume operation that you could automate. They had bits of everything; stock control, purchasing, transport, order processing, production scheduling – and all low volume stuff. We were really having to work hard, trying to make out an economic case. When you threw in the payroll, you knew you were having to scrape the barrel. Anyway, we estimated the clerical savings. All told, they were about half what was needed to justify the computer's cost. And we put up a report to the board, saying the thing wasn't on. Well, they didn't like it. They said "Weren't there any other benefits, apart from saving clerks?" Then the computer salesman suggested a formula for measuring the benefit of improved management information. Stock-outs were a big problem for this client. "Better information on inventory levels has to be worth one per cent of turnover at least," he said. Well, that swung the balance. It was just playing with figures; but they bought the argument. And against our advice. It made you realize how eager management were to be persuaded in those days.'

"By 1970, some installations had ten or more years experience. We were then able to demonstrate that programming would cost as much or more than the hardware. And that depreciation over seven years wasn't on – the type of technical advances being made then could produce a risk of obsolescence in three years. And worst of all, the rate of change meant the early customers were pioneering the hardware most of the time. But it made no difference. Clients didn't want to hear about the tangible pitfalls. They just wanted to be told about what became known as the "Intangible Benefits". And the salesmen weren't slow to realize that, since they were intangible, it didn't matter how exaggerated they were!'

But what will intrigue historians in the future, looking back over the beginnings of this second phase of the industrial revolution, is why the pragmatists were so tolerant of the enthusiasts.

Did this happen in phase one, in the eighteenth century, when we started to use machines to replace human and animal muscle? The record implies not. Luddites destroyed the machines, factory reformers constrained their use, and the whole thing was driven by good, sound Economics. If you were a successful mill owner at the time, you might well have expressed it as 'good, sound Profit'.

The astonishing thing about today's second phase, this use of machines to replace not brawn but brain, is that either we haven't tried too hard to manage the exercise in a businesslike fashion, or the traditional business planning and control methods don't work in this new area.

Case

Another manufacturing company decided, in 1971, to employ a centralized computer, located in its head office, to process its routine order processing procedures. The chief accountant had prepared the detailed proposal, on which the decision was based. He used traditional 'return on investment' techniques. His argument was that this technique was the most suitable for large, one-off expenditures. He estimated the cost, based on equipment requirements and systems development times put forward by three computer suppliers. The benefits were calculated as the clerks saved by transferring their work onto the computer, and an assessment of the return on the capital released by the reduction in both debtors and lost containers facilitated by improved data processing. These cost and revenue streams were prepared as a cash flow statement, showing that a break-even point would be reached in 3.2 years. In the event, the systems took five years to implement, the computer costs escalated to nearly three times the original estimate, no clerks were saved, and the debtors level increased – since the computer system now charged for missing containers, which held up the payment of many accounts.

The exercise had been controlled using traditional project control techniques, which again seemed perfectly reasonable. Estimating for the various activities, however, was made difficult in the absence of established norms of performance. Worse, progress could not be measured since there appeared to be no intermediate deliverables. Until a program was actually written, it was a matter of opinion what had been achieved. Even then, the quality of the program could not be measured until it was tested. Which meant waiting until all the other programs were written, and then running them all in parallel with the existing system and comparing results.

In spite of this history of disaster, the project was considered a success. 'The increase in the size of the debtors is unfortunate,' said the chief accountant. 'But we are doing so many things today that would have been impossible without the computer. We were never able to keep track of our containers before. And our turnover has doubled; which, Marketing say, owes a lot to the new discount and sales incentive scheme. This couldn't have been implemented under the old clerical system. And we have saved clerks really. Because the complexity and volume of today's paperwork would have meant employing three times as many clerks, if we hadn't had the computer system. And we know we couldn't get them. People won't do what is essentially boring, routine work anymore.'

Questioned about the project delays, he said 'We never properly specified what it was we wanted in the first place. So we were always chasing a moving target. And the equipment wasn't up to it. We only found that out as we got deeper into the work. The system needs a rewrite. Next time, we shall use one of the Database Management Systems which are now being offered. That will overcome the duplications and inconsistencies in our files, which was really our main problem.'

So it went on. We bought the databases. And then, as soon as we were offered them, second and third and even fourth generation computer languages. And on-line terminals, and distributed intelligence, and an extravagance of mips and bytes and bits and bobs until IT began to rival the energy sector as the world's number one industry.

It certainly held the all-time record for growth. So used did it become to expansion that anything less than a 50% increase in revenue year-on-year produced survival difficulties for such unfortunates on the joyride.

But it did not go on for ever. In 1985, a quite extraordinary thing happened.

In the late seventies, Price Waterhouse had established a worldwide panel of 5000 IT executives, pledged to volunteering their opinions on important IT issues. Each year they were asked what they expected their company's investment in computers to be. And each year, they expected it to be more than the last year. History showed they were right. Ever since the first computer started its business career in the fifties, every year has shown an increase in the average company's IT investment.

Until 1985 that is. Suddenly the opinion panel reported a cutback. It was unprecedented. It appeared that the boss was crying 'halt'. The annual increase was not going through 'on the nod', as in previous years. And it was not just in one country and in one industry sector. The whole western world, it seemed, had had enough of computer cost escalation.

Why everyone should decide to take a tough line at the same time is hard to explain. There was no worldwide recession that year. IT spend had, anyway, shown itself immune to recession in the past. It was a working example of the collective unconscious which must have delighted those of Jung's supporters who were monitoring hardware sales at the time. Sadly, those that there were did not inform the computer manufacturers; who also ignored the Price Waterhouse panel's prediction, and were caught unsuitably dressed for the first IT slump in history.

Its timing may be hard to explain. But the cause is now clear. For the first time, the pragmatists took their stand against the enthusiasts. For a while they won hands down. Figure 1.1 shows that IT investment levels for the average company in the ten countries surveyed, adjusted for inflation, did not recover to its 1985 level in real terms for four lean years.

What happened during these four years, and indeed, has been happening ever since, was a determined effort by management to get a handle on IT spend, and to rid itself for ever of the we/they atmosphere which had grown up between the technocrats, the management services department, the people who could drive computers; and the users of these machines, that is the company itself.

Three distinct stages in this battle of the pragmatists to get at least on equal footing with the enthusiasts are clearly charted by the Opinion Survey results.

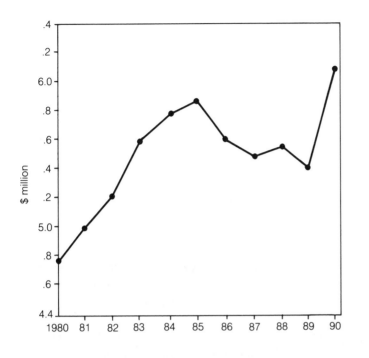

Figure 1.1   Average growth in IT spend (Japan, Australia, US and Europe).
[Source: *IT Review*, Price Waterhouse]

Firstly, there has been an emphasis on Cost Containment. The old style DP manager, whose main role was to explain the computer, has been replaced by a person whose position depends on being able to explain the computer budget. In 1983, 41% of companies had no measure of efficiency. By 1988 this had dropped to 12%, and, in that same year, 69% of chief executives expressed themselves satisfied, or largely satisfied, with the efficiency of their installations.

Simply containing costs however is to fight IT enthusiasm unjustifiably: with IT permeating the world, it is flying in the face of an irresistible wind, and one from whose strength we can surely draw profit. It soon exposes the real issue, which is measuring the 'value' for each tightly controlled dollar spent.

Now this question of 'value for money' has proved to be the big one to answer. Established accountancy measures have failed to provide the solution.

Only the users can say if they get value from the company computer, runs a popular argument. If this is true, a neat solution is to charge them for the services they receive.

Chargeback systems are becoming today's panacea. Reconstitute the IT department as IT Inc., with its own revenue stream, and its profits can demonstrably lay the spectre of 'value for money' for ever.

But isn't this all a bit artificial? Undoubtedly such systems make the user more cost conscious. So much of IT's cost is shared however, rather than attributable to a single revenue stream, that many dispute whether what the users are forced to pay represents their vote on value received.

In practice it can have quite the reverse effect. As one chief executive complained:

> 'Charging the user fobs off the problem of value for IT money onto the operating areas of the company, instead of resting it on the heads of the strategy planners where it belongs. Our main problem is the integration of IT with the rest of the company. But charging the users for costs they can't control is actually divisive.'

So much for stage one. Stage two in the 'value for money' battle, was to move the computer into areas where it could capture or defend market share – and thus be seen to be a contributor to results.

Encouraged by Professor Michael Porter's excellent missionary work, which described how American Airlines and the American Hospital Supplies Company dramatically increased the bottom-line figure on their operating statements by tying-in their customers through the imaginative use of IT, everyone started to think in terms of gaining competitive edge from their massive computer investments.

There is no need to record the two cases here; they have passed into computer folklore.

There may, however, be some point in recording that attempts to emulate these successes have resulted in great frustration for much of IT's management, and a quite extraordinary search for 'how-to-do-it' methodologies; though why a methodology for achieving competitive advantage should exist for IT, and for no other area of business, is hard to understand.

So the good news that computers weren't just an addition to the overheads – that they could actually bring in profit – was followed rapidly by the bad news that these profitable applications were tough to find.

This was recorded dramatically by a change in the IT executive's 'top problems' chart. For ten years, the opinion panel reported their chief worry was 'Meeting Project Deadlines'. But in 1987 they stopped worrying so much about making the machine work and showed a quite new concern, which was to make it work for the company.

The new concern, 'Integrating IT with Corporate Objectives', entered the charts that year. By 1988, it had become the new number one. Figure 1.2 shows it has remained among the IT executive's top problems ever since.

So there stand the pragmatists. Nothing could be more worthy than to seek a measurable, and thus manageable, return on the investment of capital, effort and skill. But nothing could be harder, it seems, when it comes to the field of Information Technology.

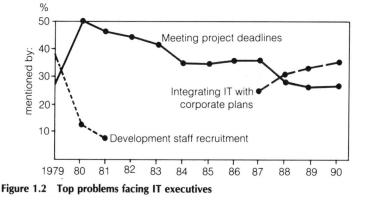

Figure 1.2   Top problems facing IT executives
[**Source:** *IT Review*, Price Waterhouse]

The third stage therefore, in the effort to gain profitable management control over the use of IT has been to appoint a person at board level, with responsibility for integrating IT and corporate objectives. In 1983, 20% of top IT executives in the world reported to the chief executive. By 1990, the number had risen to 42%. A survey of chief executives' intentions showed that, by the end of 1992, 66% of the world's leading companies intended to have an IT director.

The survey makes it clear that, faced with the intractable questions of value for money, and how to migrate the computer out of the back shop, where it was never going to set the world on fire, and into the front line of the business, the chief executives of the world's leading companies are in no doubt that IT has to be managed at board level. The fact that so few existing IT executives expect to get there leaves some doubt as to where these directors will come from.

The move is well under way however. A recent survey of the UK's top 500 companies showed 74% have appointed a director with the specific responsibility of integrating IT within business strategy. It is not always his sole responsibility, but in each case it is a clear one, and in 90% of cases it is a new responsibility, incorporated at board level within the last three years.

In 1989, Price Waterhouse, in collaboration with the Financial Times, set up a new Opinion Panel in the UK, with members all drawn from these new appointments to the board. It is of interest to note that of these IT directors, 37% did not have IT as their main background, and came from Production, Marketing and Accounting disciplines.

But still, the argument rages: should a provider of administration

Cases

services ever have a seat on the board? If so, isn't it just a temporary appointment, until the great IT difficulty is sorted out?

During the research, described later in the chapter, case studies showed that three distinct views on the subject of IT directors prevail. The first is typified by the statement 'Boards employ specialists. They are not specialists themselves.' The view is that the top IT executive's job is to provide the IT infrastructure on which today's organization depends. It is a big job, because the cost of this infrastructure is so big. But it does not merit a board appointment. Because it is unconnected with strategy. The IT infrastructure, on its own, cannot affect revenue streams and earnings per share. The applications, which may support corporate strategy, are hung onto this infrastructure, but they are the responsibility of the user functions.

The second view, argued equally forcibly, is exactly the reverse. It is not just the size of the investment that makes the job big. It is the fundamental importance of sound IT strategy to the fortunes of the company. Security, attractiveness as an employer, participating effectively in IT business cultures which are beginning to dominate in all activities, getting these things right is fundamental to survival. At the least, boards need an IT director in the role similar to the one of protection exercised by company secretaries. At the best, with IT becoming the dominant strategic weapon, the IT director will have more influence over revenue streams than anyone else. Production, Finance and Marketing have each, in turn, been the leading influence on organizational strategy. They are all still vital functions. But provided the IT director is prepared to accept responsibility for the business results of IT strategies, and not just the technical achievement, no organization can afford not to have the IT director as part of the top executive team.

The third argument is, in effect, something of a compromise. It goes: 'IT is not attached to a revenue stream. When it does form a vital component of business strategy, there is always some user function that has prime responsibility for that strategy. Long term therefore, IT directors will pass away. But we have been subjected to some awful mistakes; costly mistakes pioneering technology, costly disasters when the systems went wrong, and missed opportunities because no one saw the computer's potential. We can't afford to be under a technical department's tyranny again. We're making an appointment to the board with responsibility for integrating IT with business direction, to get this thing right once and for all. We see it as a three to five year appointment. Once the right foundations are laid, the users will be able to run with the thing.'

The long honeymoon is over. Value for money is now the watch cry. On the board or not, and in both the short and long term, the top IT executive's job has to be concerned with measuring the return on the computer investment.

But it is frequently held that established accountancy measures have failed to provide any suitable yardstick. Why is this? Is there something wrong with accounting techniques? Or is there something so different about computers that they just won't respond to the auditor's stethoscope? A bit of both, it seems.

Admittedly, we don't know the return we'll get from any investment, in computers or in anything else. We can't be certain. But the thing we've invested in has a purpose. It may not work as we hoped. We can define its purpose, however. And if the purpose is achieved, we can say how much better off we'll be.

Can't we?

If we can't, what are we doing investing all that money in the first place?

Well, the argument goes, computers are a bit different. They have a purpose. But their purpose isn't to produce a benefit. It's to enable someone else to get one.

'OK,' says your businessman, not at all discouraged by this, 'Let's measure the benefit this someone else is going to get.'

'Ah! You can't actually. You see, it's intangible.'

Now the businessman has never seen an intangible benefit. He doubts if anyone else has.

'That's right. You can't see them. But we go for them all the time. A new office block, a new canteen. There's no direct payoff, the benefits are intangible. But we all know they're there.'

At this point, another question seems in order. Do we all know they're there? The businessman will have questioned, times without number, the worthwhileness of all that prestige office rent, and the nouvelle cuisine that the canteen manager is turning out.

It seems the accountancy profession has rather let go of this one. Indirect costs they are happy with. They are costs that are not directly related to the product. They can be charged to the products on some arbitrary basis. Or they can be lumped together as overheads, and deducted from the profit at the end of the day.

But indirect benefits! Well, if there are indirect costs, there must be indirect benefits. But what's the point of trying to measure them? What's the point of attempting to measure the benefits of having a head office or a canteen, when we've devised a perfectly satisfactory way of absorbing the costs in the first place? If they're making too big a dint in the profit, we can consider a spot of rationalization. Otherwise, leave well alone.

This argument should not be unduly criticized, since it has stood the test of time. That is, until the computer came along. Then we discovered a whole string of differences between the computer and a head office block. Consider these.

Perception of role Most indirect investments (offices, administration systems, canteens) are considered to be good things, important things to the business. But no one ever suggests they are profit earners. No investment in computers was ever made however, without first preparing a statement showing, not just the costs, but also the hoped-for benefits.

Shared contribution These hoped-for benefits are shown to result from a new data processing or communications system. The system rarely produces the benefits on its own however. Production, purchasing, marketing or distribution have to play their part. Increased profit may be directly attributable, but not solely attributable, to the computer.

Fuzzy contribution If the benefit is not the automation of a specific process, then it is the contribution made to profits by the provision of better information. But what is information worth? The calculation is fuzzy, since it depends on the use some human being may make of it.

Necessity At a pinch, we can do without the canteen. But in 25 short years, every sizeable organization in the world has become totally dependant on its IT systems for survival.

Cost The key difference is the sheer size of the bill. At five per cent of turnover, and rising, IT expenditure is just too big a sum to tuck away in the overheads.

It was suggested earlier that the nutshell purpose of this book is to address the problem of exerting bottom line control over runaway IT enthusiasm. Since this problem has become such an important matter at board level, and in view of the rush to appoint an IT director, it deals with the issue by considering the whole question of the board's involvement with IT.

It has long been a precept of clear communication that authors should say what they have to say, say it, and then say what they have said. We spare the reader a final summary. But four important insights into the IT director's world emerged as our research progressed. They surprised us. They may not surprise the reader. But just in case, here is a warning.

- The management techniques we have developed in business over the last 200 years do not seem to work properly when applied to computers.

- A large number of IT directors, and in the world's largest companies, are frankly worried about the possibility of an 'out of control' situation.

- IT defines a new role for the chief executive.

- Nearly all IT directors are unable to persuade their senior colleagues of what they believe is the role of the computer, and are implementing IT strategies by means of a *hidden agenda*.

The book is in three parts. Part I is introductory. Part II discusses the role of executives responsible for IT at board level. What are the questions which should be resolved there; should an IT director have responsibility for business results; who takes the initiative in planning IT strategies, who takes the initiative in identifying IT applications; is the IT director a promoter, opening the eyes of the board to the potential of the IT revolution, or a protector, concerned that nothing in the business shall be put in jeopardy by the onrush of the new technology – or even a peacemaker, just there to break down some of the behavioural issues which have grown up around what some have called the Beast of Business?

Perhaps a co-ordinator, a custodian of standards, responsible for the provision of an efficient IT service, and ensuring the harmonious decentralization of what many feel has been too centralized, too long?

One powerful reason for appointing an IT director, emerging from our research, was fear. Fear that IT will soon repaint the old familiar landscape in some rather strange colours. Fear that, whilst we, on this board, might not be too clear what these colours will be, some of our competitors are sure to be sorting it all out. Fear that the blandishments and pressures, from salesmen and our own staff, are sometimes exerted without that special perspective that comes from being responsible for bottom line – and since we don't know enough about it, shouldn't we have someone on the board who does, someone who will be one of us, and who we can trust?

There is nothing wrong in being motivated by well-founded fears. But, if a saviour is to be appointed, history shows the terms of reference can easily be too broad. We need to be clear about the details of the role.

Part III deals with the key IT issues that face every organization, and will grow in importance as we move into the next century. Our research shows them to be four in number.

- Firstly, the problem that has turned out to be the top worry for IT directors: how to bridge the culture gap between IT and business professionals?

- What is the proper extent of the centralization and decentralization of IT now that hardware price reductions and off-the-shelf packages have put the possibility of control into the hands of the users?

- What can be done about that most intractable of problems: getting computer systems up and running within cost budgets and on time?

- Lastly, and as a fitting conclusion, the book concentrates on the business difficulty which overlays all of the other issues. It discusses and summarizes what the research has uncovered on the key 'value for money' question. How can we measure IT benefits, and get value from the investment?

We have referred a number of times to the research which has gone into the compilation of this book. Now is perhaps the time to describe what this research was. Two types of investigation were undertaken.

Firstly, numerous surveys were undertaken of the opinions of the 5000 members of the Price Waterhouse panel of IT executives running computer installations throughout the world, and of the specially constituted panel of 100 UK IT directors, founded jointly by the Financial Times and Price Waterhouse in 1989.

It was the first of these panels, the international panel, that, in 1986, correctly forecast the swing, now materializing, to appoint IT directors to the board. The second panel was then formed to give a voice to these new directors once they had arrived, and to add another plank to the, as yet, frail bridge of understanding between businessmen and IT professionals. All the statistics quoted in the charts and in the text of this book have been drawn from specially formulated studies conducted within these two panels.*

Secondly, a large number of organizations in both the private and public sectors have opened their doors to us in order that we could investigate the IT issues they have faced and are facing at board level. We have conducted 102 face-to-face interviews with IT directors in the major IT-using countries of the world: in North America, Europe, Japan and Australia.

We have had the benefit of an editorial panel consisting of five Price Waterhouse partners, four from the IT practice and one from

---

* Unless otherwise stated, the statistics represent the average of the opinions expressed in North America, Europe, Japan and Australia.

the Human Resources discipline. Their valuable experience has guided the production of this book. In addition, they suggested many specific questions to be investigated, and provided innumerable insights.

They also managed the interview and investigation programme, selecting suitable cases from amongst their clients. Without these personal contacts, the studies of real life trials and tribulations, upon which the book entirely depends, could never have been undertaken. It is a novel thing for the board to concern itself with IT in any depth. It is a new branch of management. There is no body of knowledge. All that can be done is to study what the world's top companies are doing and experiencing, and glean from them the pitfalls and the promising paths to take.

This is what we have done. In this book there are over one hundred cases studies, drawn from the countries mentioned.

At first, we anticipated the need to write a separate section for each country. The research has shown however that every country has followed much the same path in its exploration of IT. The main differences are those of timing, and of emphasis.

In Europe, for example, France, Germany and the UK, each pioneered the use of computers in business in the early '60s. They have the same history of mistakes, and the same mature interest today in the management of IT at board level. Late entrants on a large scale, to the IT age, for example Spain, tell a good news, bad news story. The good news is that they are able to enter the information revolution armed with the latest software and hardware, and without the burdensome legacy of the cumbersome systems that the pioneers built. The bad news is that they have not yet learned from their mistakes. And, since there seems to be no other way of learning where computers are concerned, there is not the awareness of the pitfalls of rapid, uncontrolled automation, nor of the need for board-level involvement.

The US was, of course, the pioneer of the pioneers. Not by much, if at all, in the development of the technology. But in the massive application of the technology, they left Europe standing in the '60s. Cheaper hardware, and a remarkable faith that mechanization on a large scale always led to greater efficiency, encouraged them in the wholesale automation of administration processes – but largely of existing processes, without any fundamental rethinking.

It also encouraged them to value the technology kings of the pioneering era. Today, they possibly suffer the pioneering legacy more than any other country. They labour under the burden of some of the world's largest, but now old-fashioned, computer programs – and display a worrying tendency to hope that a technology will appear which will re-engineer them automatically into efficient programs which can use the latest operating systems. They also have a plethora of senior IT executives left over from the days when making computers work was the only criteria for holding their jobs. Now that the flavour has changed to making these computers work for the company, such men and women no longer fit the bill.

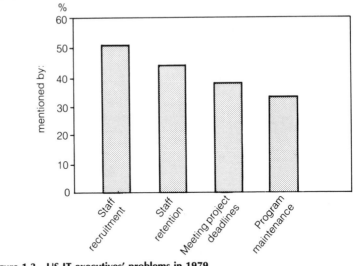

Figure 1.3 US IT executives' problems in 1979

Japan stands out as being both a late entry and as deploying a different emphasis on its use of IT. They were late in using computers probably because they didn't suffer the staff constraints of the West. In Japan, in the '60s, there was an abundance of clerical labour – educated, responsible people still prepared to do menial tasks. With little drive to automate their administration systems, they suffered correspondingly little from the programmer shortage besetting other countries. And, because the problem of systems development was not fully recognized, there was little concentration on the problem in the educational institutions and universities.

A further factor retarding recognition of automation problems in the business administration area, was the policy of Japanese hardware suppliers, keen to oust IBM from their market leader position, to supply all the software needed with each machine sold. There were very few systems developed in-house. By the eighties, Japan stood out as the flip-side of the IT coin.

Because of their heavy reliance on the use of outside contractors to develop their systems, the businesses themselves experienced acute maintenance problems (they did not understand their programs since they had not written them), but saw system development as a simple matter of calling in outsiders.

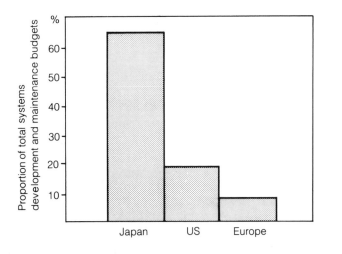

Figure 1.4   Use of outside contractors in 1980

It is only recently, for example, that there has been any strong interest in packaged software in Japan. There is still no strong swing from back shop to front shop computing. The technical difficulties of building user interfaces using Kanji characters are popularly blamed – but nearer the truth seems to be the lack of consumer demand, for IT-based banking services, and for point-of-sale applications because of small retail outlets for example. Despite the lead Japan has in producing IT hardware, there is evidence that they are suffering a ten year gap when it comes to applying it to automate administration processes.

> THE WEST WAS PIONEERING IT IN THE '60S, JAPAN IN THE '70S.
>
> THE PROGRAMMING BACKLOG IS ONLY JUST BECOMING A MAJOR DIFFICULTY AND JAPAN'S INTEREST IN SYSTEMS DEVELOPMENT PRODUCTIVITY AIDS – PACKAGES AND 4GLS – IS A RECENT PHENOMENA

A difference of IT emphasis, however, balances their neglect of administration systems, and puts Japan at the forefront when it comes to production systems. As their economy began to lead the world in heavy manufacture and electronics, concentration on CAD/CAM, robotics, AI in process control and JIT systems has made them world leaders in this area.

So much for international differences. It remains to thank all contributors, worldwide, who gave so freely of their time, and who were so astonishingly frank and open during interviews. We claim no credit for persuading them into this participation in the research. In every case we were warmed by an unusual motivation to talk, inspired, we have no doubt, by concern for what one respondent called 'the neglected area of management, but which, one day soon, will become the only area where companies compete'.

Being no more than a report of these research findings, this is a book where the author can take none of the credit for any of the lessons it may teach. It is a shame therefore, that these thanks have to be anonymous. A number of the participants made this a condition however. So, to preserve a consistent flavour, we have applied the rule to all.

We should say, at the outset, that this is not a technical book. We make no apology. There are plenty of intriguing technical issues. And plenty of technicians, solving them faster than the world can absorb.

Peter Drucker would often say it was not the intended results of inventions, but their side-effects, which really changed the world. We need look no further than the motor car for a dramatic example of this. It is already abundantly clear that mankind will be kept far busier solving the environmental problems the car creates than he ever was inventing it.

Case

Another conference, and another Guru. He was establishing the fact of the extraordinarily high progress rate achieved with Information Technology.

'If the motor car industry,' he said, 'had made the same rate of progress that we have made in the IT industry, a Rolls Royce would cost two dollars forty' – he paused dramatically, then, punching the air with his fists – 'and do a million miles to the gallon.'

Absolute silence fell on the audience. Suddenly a voice was heard from the back of the hall.

'Yes,' came the reply, 'but it would be very small!'

The side-effects of progress are unpredictable. One of the side-effects of the invention of the computer is the difficulty of harnessing it profitably to the business.

It sort of runs away with us. And suddenly, here we are, doing lots of new things, and wondering why we hadn't planned them, and whether we would have planned them, if we'd thought of them in the first place, and how we can't measure if it's been worthwhile because we can't go back anyway – and, just as suddenly, there they are, in the living room, on the desk in the board room, and stretching out their tentacles to our customers' desks, and to our suppliers, and soon they'll be talking to each other, and shouldn't we appoint someone to get all this under control, and what about an IT director?

The important issues are human issues: of enthusiasm, of attempted pragmatism, of skills and fears, of retraining and rethinking. They are management issues: of planning and control in a new world, like Einstein's, where our once-trusted rulers no longer seem to measure correctly.

If traditional management techniques are not appropriate for IT, we might also question whether traditional management objectives are. Electronics has been hailed as the first fruit of science which is not harmful to the planet. Certainly non-materialistic progress is in a state of worship by the young. And the computer, the first machine which actually does nothing, can claim great respect on this account. Should we therefore be looking for traditional returns on investment, as we move into the world of information?

No one is going to propose that we overturn our economics on the computer's account. All anyone encountered in our research suggested, is that it needs some adjustment. If this book eschews the technicalities of IT, and concentrates on the human and management issues raised, we shall certainly not have picked a trivial subject. The questions we asked of our participants in the research were, in fact, nothing short of 'how should we manage our way into phase two of the Industrial Revolution?'

The book is peppered with cases and quotations; all obeying the rule of anonymity for the reasons stated, but perhaps more telling because of that. There are IT disasters, management mistakes and confessions of doubt in these pages, which might have been toned down, or evaporated completely, if they had to be attributed.

But rules are allowed their one exception. Sir Denys Henderson, Chairman of ICI, one of the world's largest multinationals, confessed to a major concern about IT when he learned this research was about to be undertaken. It is a most telling statement, from one of the IT industry's biggest customers. We are grateful for his permission to reproduce it.

Unwittingly at the time, but now, hopefully, with some satisfaction, he set the scene for much of this book. How far it meets his concern is not for this chapter. But at least it takes his question head on. He said:

'I still worry enormously, both about the amount we spend on IT and the increasing difficulty of justifying that expense in terms of the bottom line. In the end, I think that this will work to the disadvantage of the suppliers of hardware, software and systems because simply to say "Can you afford not to spend when you look at your competitors?" or alternatively, "There is hidden commercial advantage that is unquantifiable" will quite frankly not be enough in future.'

Part 2

IT AT BOARD LEVEL

❝There is no point in being made aware of costs unless you can do something about them❞

❝Once it was all about trade, the days of the great merchants. Then it was about production, and the engineer was king. When the critical path became raising and deploying capital, the accountant held sway. Recently, consumerism has brought the marketeer to power. In the future, it's clear that power and success will accompany the management of information resources. Right now however, when it comes to an involvement with the new information technology, businessmen won't participate. They say 'Tell us!' But, in the end, there is only one person they'll listen to – one of themselves❞

Chapter 2

Why appoint an IT director?

&&Nobody outside of the board will ever have that much power again**,,**

Section 1
Cost escalation

❝ My appointment was the first recognition that there was a major investment in IT – that it was out of control – and that there was a desperate need to get a handle on the thing ❞

❝ The brief from the board was 'Look at the size of the spend and see if we're getting a business benefit – and please, don't spend any more.' The view of the board was 'It's all sitting there wasting money, isn't it? ❞

❝ Here, and world-wide, was a sudden consciousness by boards that we were in a runaway spend situation and that someone should get a hold of it. But the last person to do that was the technician, who was driven by spending more and more ❞

The revolution began very quietly. A new machine was invented for scientists and engineers to do their sums better. It was the absence of any moving parts that was new. It worked electronically, potentially at the speed of light.

It seems to be a law of progress that machines designed for one purpose become mainly used for something else. The steam engine which originally pumped water, later revolutionised transport. This new computing engine, designed to perform calculations, soon became used to automate a host of information processing tasks undertaken by humans.

A world war hastened its development for soldiers to aim their guns better. The machine was then stolen by a small number of visionary business people, who believed it could process their payrolls better.

This theft took place in the mid-1950s. It was obvious that a machine which could work out the trajectory of an explosive shell could handle the simple 'hours worked times rate of pay' type of calculations needed. But what these pioneers of information technology also saw was that, because the computer could be programmed, it could be taught all the processes that their payroll clerks performed.

And because it had a memory to hold its program, and all the mysterious 'workings out' that delight mathematicians, so it could store and retrieve the things accountants like to have around them – employee's records and tax tables and suchlike.

But the moment that cheque was signed for the first consignment of hardware, management was trapped. The trap worked like this.

As ever, the biggest constraint on getting things done was getting people to do them. An obedient machine to replace a wilful workforce was an attractive proposition. Largely on the say-so of the suppliers, boards of directors throughout the world authorised the purchase of a computer.

They knew nothing of the machine's capabilities however, or how to make it work. So they employed specialists – a whole departmentful: data entry clerks, computer operators, programmers, systems analysts and an IT executive to look after them.

This new IT department drove the computer. But mainly it produced programs, the software without which the computer would not work.

The need for this programming activity, particularly the need for so much of it, surprised the board. The cost of the software began to rival what they'd spent on the hardware.

But now it was their own staff, not the suppliers, who were advising them. 'If you want it to work, we have to write these programs,' they were told. The board was trapped. They could pull out, or sign more cheques.

Very soon they felt a further turn of the screw. Their data processing department told them that the machine they'd bought wasn't man enough for the job. It was underspecified.

'Nobody's fault. How can you know these things until you try it out? But now we can see how it performs – and we need double the memory to hold the programs, three more tape units and an extra printer.'

More cheques were signed.

And then, another turn!

'I'm afraid the original statement of user requirements was way, way too thin. Again, nobody's fault. I guess people don't know what they want until you give them something. And then they only know what they don't want. The fact is, those 42 programs the manufacturers said we'd have to write just don't cover the ground. We're now looking at the need for around 200.'

And yet another! The technology was in its infancy. Orders of magnitude improvements in processing power were being achieved every three or four years. They still are. More important, new ways of doing things were produced: new communication systems connecting computers to terminals, and then to each other; new automatic operating systems and computer languages; new data capture and storage devices; new ways of displaying information.

The pressure to take advantage of each wave of progress, so obviously an improvement on what they had, was hard for the board to resist. It's no surprise either that such resistance has never been encouraged by their technical advisers, where professional challenges, and the opportunities for more experience, unavoidably play their part.

These four causes:

- The difficulty of estimating and controlling software development costs

- The failure to appreciate how much hardware will be required

- Coming to grips with users' requirements as the system is being built instead of before work starts

- Hardware and software which becomes technically obsolete every three to four years

have lead to an information technology cost escalation problem which has affected every computer installation in the world. For many years, it was a problem top management felt powerless to control.

Case

The president of a large US company, manufacturing and distributing food, had inherited, on succeeding to the chief executive position, an IT department whose annual costs amounted to 4% of turnover. Determined to improve efficiency generally in the company, he had instituted economy measures in all other departments and was now planning expansion, by re-investing in the most profitable activities. The IT department had defeated all his attempts to reduce their budget however. At the same time, they had been unable to provide any convincing statement of business benefits for each dollar spent. The department was run by the accounting vice-president since most of the early applications had been in his responsibility area. The president felt that, as a non-technician, the accountant was possibly dominated by the arguments of his specialist staff. He appointed a man from outside the company to head up the department therefore, a person with a strong background in the computer field, and gave him the brief of auditing the spend and making savings where possible. After six months, the new computer manager reported that the department was saddled with out-of-date technology, and that maintaining it, and struggling to make it process ever-increasing data volumes, had put the department on a dangerous 'diminishing returns' curve. There was nowhere to go with their present computer, he said. It was at the top of its range. A new generation computer was needed. It would mean spending more initially, but it was much faster, and had the expansion capacity to cope with the future needs of the business. The president could not verify any part of these proposals for himself, nor could he bring himself to trust a newcomer with so important a decision. He therefore called in consultants to corroborate the recommendation. They spent time examining the needs of the business. In their report, they rejected the new manager's proposal since it involved reprogramming all the company's systems, which they argued would be too costly, time-consuming and not feasible with the present programming team. Instead, they proposed keeping the existing machine, but decentralizing much of the work to satellite computers in the depots and stores. This proposal also meant increasing the computer department spend rather that containing it. The consultants justified their recommendation on grounds of survival, pointing out that local computer processing was the way retail business would be done in the future. The computer manager then defended his original proposal, saying that although the programs would need to be rewritten, this would be done using a new 'fourth generation' language, which would make the operation fast and cheap.

'It wasn't that either of these proposals was necessarily wrong,' said the president. 'It was us, in the executive suite, that were wrong. None of us had the knowledge or the experience to get hold of the IT operation ourselves. None of us had accepted the responsibility for getting a payoff. We were relying on outsiders – consultants, or technicians who were on our staff, but quite frankly, always seemed to have more interest in computing than the business. We didn't know what to do. And when you don't know, you have to rely on someone you can trust. I trust the guys who run the company with me. We've fought a lot of business battles together, and they put their heads on the block each time. In this case we found ourselves preferring the view of the consultants to that of our manager – but they weren't going to be around to shoulder the payoff.'

The graph in Figure 2.1 shows the average spend, worldwide, on information technology by data processing departments.

The figures reveal an uninterrupted increase of some 6% each year, until 1985. The increase appears to be impervious to the ups and downs of trade conditions.

Remember, these are average figures. For many larger companies, their IT budgets were ten times the average, or more. It was, in the end, the sheer size of the spend that alerted boards to the uncontrolled leak in their budgetary control systems.

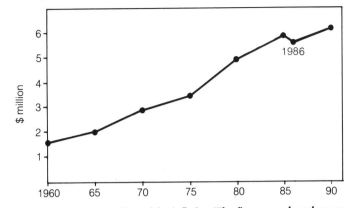

Figure 2.1   average IT spend, adjusted for inflation [The figures are based on an analysis of Price Waterhouse clients' spend until 1979 when the computer survey was founded.]

Why did the figure dip in 1985, and then remain relatively steady?

Case

In 1984, a European-based multinational manufacturing pharmaceuticals analysed its IT expenditure as a result of growing concern in all subsidiaries throughout the early 1980s that computer hardware and software costs were approaching 5% of total expenditure. A specially constituted study group reported four common factors discovered in each company:

1) Peaks of cost escalation were related more to the suppliers' announcements of new equipment than to any noticeable increase in company needs.
2) Despite continual announcements of order of magnitude improvements in cost/performance achieved in computer technology, there was no evidence of these being passed on as cost reductions to their computer departments. Instead, each technical breakthrough seemed to be absorbed by pressures for more capacity, communications, storage and applications both by computer staff and the users.
3) There were no measures of efficiency in any of their computer departments.
4) Expenditure was proposed and controlled, in all cases, by people under pressure to provide a better data processing service but not for achieving business results.

It was decided that all four symptoms pointed to a lack of board level control. One of the existing main board directors was given an additional responsibility for IT control throughout the group.

With hindsight, the statistics show that this company typified world-wide concern and reaction at this particular time in computer history. Why everyone reacted at about the same time is not clear. The fact that microcomputers became commonplace in both the office and home helped the board to lose its fear of challenging the technical arguments supporting cost escalation. Perhaps it was the further fact that escalation had been accumulating at much the same rate in all companies since 1960, and resulted in their IT costs reaching 'critical mass' at the same time. At first, the concern was not manifested in the appointment of IT directors. That came later. But in 1985 two things were achieved, which paved the way:

- One aspect of IT at least, its cost, was recognised as a matter for the board.
- Following board pressure, IT management assumed a new business-oriented look, and technical knowledge was no longer the main criterion for survival or promotion.

IN 1983 48% OF COMPUTER INSTALLATIONS HAD NO MEASURE OF EFFICIENCY. BY 1988 THIS HAD FALLEN TO 12%.

IN 1986 A COMPUTER PERFORMANCE MEASUREMENT GROUP WAS FORMED IN THE UK WITH 11 MEMBERS. BY 1989 THE MEMBERSHIP WAS 1100.

IN 1987 'COST CONTAINMENT' ENTERED THE TOP FOUR IN THE IT EXECUTIVES' PROBLEMS CHART, MENTIONED BY 28% OF INSTALLATIONS.

IN 1990, 28% OF IT DIRECTORS GAVE 'COST CONTROL' AS THE MAIN REASON FOR THEIR APPOINTMENT

❝ I did no more than introduce the same sort of controls we use in every other department. It was the attitude change that really did the trick **❞**

Section 2
Systems development problems

66 Programming always takes double what you think, even when you've doubled it 99

66 As a programming manager, you need to rewrite Parkinson's Law. Programming work expands to fill the capacity of the computer enhancement you were foolish enough to mention, this year's budget plus any of next year's you can bring forward, and the user's patience to bursting 99

66 The world's programming backlog is estimated at 15 million programmer years. With one and a half million programmers chasing it, it's still in sight. But there's a ghost backlog of systems the users don't dare ask for any more. No one can see that far 99

In 1979, Price Waterhouse formed the panel of IT executives who were to chart world opinion on computer management issues for the next decade and more. The first survey led with the question 'What is the major issue facing you right now?' Staff Recruitment came back the answer. 52% of the panel said their main difficulty was attracting and retaining the systems analysts and programmers they needed to meet the demand for computer systems flooding in from the users.

To be an experienced programmer in those days, or at any time in the previous 20 years, was virtually to command your own price. The world was intent on automating every factory job and office task in sight. The biggest constraint on progress with this objective had turned out to be, not the technology, the power and proficiency of the computers available, but our astonishing ineptitude at programming them.

Without programs telling them what to do, the computers would, of course, do nothing. Many did just that. For some years after they were purchased.

Once they were got going, the users, who hadn't warmed too much to the prospect of being automated when it was first mooted, now discovered that the computer didn't do what they wanted anyway.

The systems analysts had got hold of the wrong end of the stick, the programmers had dropped it and, seemingly, found one of their own – and, truth to tell, the users hadn't really known what they wanted in the first place.

So there were a host of alterations to do. And, as the users began to appreciate the possibilities of automation, and could usually lose the costs in the overheads, more and more applications found their way onto the waiting list.

Demand for those who could talk the computer's language took off in unsatisfiable proportions.

But there was just a limited number of experienced programmers in the world. And they were being harried from installation to installation with the offer of bigger and bigger salaries.

> 66 When we installed our first computer, I formed a steering committee of the heads of all the user departments, to try to generate some enthusiasm. By 1980, I had to reconstitute it as a rationing committee. Demand had just got out of hand 99

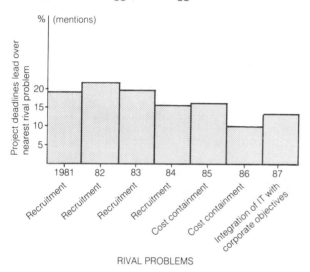

Figure 2.2 'Meeting project deadlines' compared with rival problems

Figure 2.2 shows that, one year after the survey started, IT executives gave up on recruitment to solve their problems. The whole management task of systems development took over as the number one worry. This included staffing – but embraced retraining in-house staff, the possibility of sub contracting the work, programming methods, estimating and control methods and the use of pre-written programs or 'packages'.

To top management, the whole issue resolved itself into one of 'meeting project deadlines'. And that was the name of the new number one in the problems chart. It was to stay there as the top worry for seven years.

Why did the problem prove to be so intractable?

Case

A public transport company in Europe, one of the earliest users of computers, found meeting project deadlines for new computer systems to be the most serious factor inhibiting the implementation of their plans. After studying experience in several other countries, they presented their findings at an international project management conference in 1984. Their conclusion was that the combined effect of three factors distinguished programming from other activities undertaken in business, and made the task of building bespoke computer systems, using the 'separate applications' approach then current, unmanageable within prescribed cost and delivery targets. The three factors they identified were:

> ❝ When I first became software manager, I used to wonder why it always failed. Now, I wonder why it ever works ❞

The nature of the work   Programming is intrinsically difficult. They cited a typical system which contained 110 thousand opportunities to go one way or another in the program. The system interfaced with 25 other systems, each of similar complexity. Work out the combinatorial possibilities of making a mistake, they said, and the figure runs out of the window. It is impossible to check anything rigorously beyond 500 lines of code. Most organisations have systems each running into a million or so lines. It is also difficult to estimate the work involved since every computer system breaks new ground. It will be the first time all, or part of, the system has been processed automatically and not according to human discretion, and both the requirements and the feasibility of the computer to automate the work evolve as the project progresses. 'You're always shooting at a moving target,' they said. Furthermore, control of the human and technical resources is difficult since they are 'foreign' to the business, and outside the experience range of most of the company's management.

> ❝ When I investigated why we couldn't get any new systems off the ground, I discovered 80% of the programmers were tied up maintaining the old ones ❞

The interference of maintenance   No program is ever finished. It will always contain errors which only later come to light. And it must be alive, in the sense that the business it serves is alive, and constantly changing. But, because of the logical complexity of programs, changes are hard to make, and the more you make, the harder they get. Each change has unexpected effects. And it's no good telling programmers not to write 'spaghetti' programs. It is in the nature of nervous systems to have many interconnections. And that is what we are building – a nervous system for the business. The maintenance problem is worsened by the roving nature of the workforce, who can easily increase their salary by joining a new company and are never around when their programs need maintaining. And by most programmers' dislike of maintenance, which they find irksome compared with the creativity of starting a new program on a clean sheet of paper.

The short-term/long-term conflict   The business wants short-term benefits. We are used to making plans for this year – two years at most. But in IT we can't build soundly that fast. If we do – using packages for instance, or letting the users 'go-it-alone', – we pay a price. Piecemeal development takes place. When we later want the benefits IT can give us of integrating the organization, of supporting projects that cut across departmental boundaries, of setting up a common communication system which draws on a common database, these are no longer open to us. Yet it is outside the practice of most businesses to authorise the sort of long-term investment that is needed in IT to build the necessary infrastructures, but against which no clear identifiable payoff can be offset.

This pessimistic view that the task was being tackled in the wrong way, a view privately held by many IT executives, was not accepted overtly. Instead, a plethora of tools for writing these wrong sort of programs faster has been put on the market.

Some, notably the tailorable package, and its close relative, the 'fourth generation language', have provided order of magnitude improvements in productivity.

Case

The Chief Information Officer of a large insurance company in the US had been appointed to run the information systems department in 1961, and had held the position, as it grew in importance, for thirty years. He recounted the history of 'panaceas' for solving the systems development problem that his company had tried in that time.
'I see it as three waves of techniques,' he said. 'Each wave was worshipped for about a decade. In the 60s, we pinned our faith on better languages – the 'let's talk to the computer the way we talk to each other' movement, which produced the so-called 2nd generation and 3rd generation languages and made progressively more and more use of English. In the 70s we started to use operating packages. We didn't call them that – we called them operating systems and database management systems. But they were packages, pre-written programs to solve the problems that bugged programmers most: getting the machine to access their programs and access the data. In the 80s, we called ourselves 'systems engineers' and started to use some basic engineering techniques; templating, building models and prototyping. Fourth generation languages appeared, which basically assembled suitable templates together. And CASE tools [Computer Aided Systems Engineering], for modelling and prototyping, and sometimes even generating finished programs. Each wave lifted us a little higher,' he claimed. 'But the combined effect of the whole lot together didn't get us onto the shore. Meeting project deadlines is still our major problem.'

> ❝ We're just getting further and further apart. It used to take two to three years to build the average system. Today, with networks, databases and external system interfaces to think about, it takes nearer five. But the business planning horizon has dropped from two years to three months ❞

One should not decry the achievement of project deadlines – to have remained unattainable since computer-time began, despite the undeniably formidable array of suitors questing ways to meet her: all the world's computer manufacturers, software suppliers, IT consultants and IT managers.

Just what have we accomplished? The improvement of the tools used for programming has had three main effects:

1   The productivity of programmers has increased – by about threefold in the case of general programs; but incalculably in cases where standard solutions are acceptable. In these cases, the fourth generation language's 'template' approach really comes into its own. Application packages can also be used. Sometimes these packages provide instant, off-the-shelf solutions. Sometimes they need tailoring, but still they represent major shortcuts.

> IN 1988, 36% OF ALL PROGRAMS WERE ESTIMATED TO HAVE BEEN BOUGHT IN AS PACKAGES.

2   Some programming work has been deskilled. Programs which need to exploit the intricacies of the technology still demand skill and experience. But, where standard solutions are acceptable and fourth generation languages and packages can be used, less skill is required, and users can frequently provide their own systems.
3   Side by side with the users' ability to provide their own systems has arisen a trend to decentralisation, and to a by-passing of the traditional centralised computer department.

> BY 1993, IT EXECUTIVES ESTIMATE THAT 75% OF ALL PROGRAMMING WILL BE DONE BY THE USERS OR BY PROGRAMMERS UNDER THE USERS' CONTROL.
>
> IN 1990 THE PROBLEM OF GO-IT-ALONE USERS HAD GROWN FROM NEGLIGIBLE PROPORTIONS TO BECOME THE MAIN CONCERN OF 17% OF IT EXECUTIVES.

It is the go-it-alone statistic that gives a clue to today's deadlines problem.

Another clue comes from the growing use of outside contractors to undertake systems development work.

❝ If we use contractors, which is where the experience and ability is today, we lose control ❞

> BY 1990, CONTRACTORS WERE RESPONSIBLE FOR 23% OF ALL SYSTEMS DEVELOPMENT WORK IN EUROPE, 28% IN AUSTRALIA, 32% IN THE US AND 62% IN JAPAN.

However, the willy-nilly use of contractors without a policy defining where this is desirable, without an in-house systems architect planning contracted work so that it forms part of an integrated design, without thorough inspection of the work and a tight contract specifying delivery standards, may help to meet a short-term deadline at the cost of putting long-term deadlines in jeopardy.

The key to the systems development problem, as it manifests itself today, is to be found in the 'wrong approach' mentioned in the first case study.

The corporate need in the 90s, and for the foreseeable future, is for integrated systems. This springs from:

- Project management, which cuts across departmental boundaries to meet corporate objectives, replacing the old style of hierarchical management
- Total quality control methods
- Moves towards vertical integration to remove inefficient 'cushions' in the value chain
- Moves towards horizontal integration in the sales area to exploit the full range of services during a single sales opportunity
- Executive information systems, which also cut across departmental boundaries
- The increasing pace of change in business requirements, which means that computer systems need to be evolved, rather than produced in a fixed and final state.

We saw in the previous section (cost escalation) that 1985 was a Watershed year; a year in which, encouraged by board level insistence, the emphasis in IT management shifted from exploiting the technology to serving the business.

In the area of systems development, the main concern since Watershed is systems segregation and their consequent inflexibility. All the key trends led to it: packages, contractors, speeded-up delivery and decentralisation – all encouraged separate 'standalone' applications, constructed in the apparent belief that the users knew what they wanted, and would never change their minds. The old style of programming forced it: the custom of tackling one application at a time – each with its own files, without the ability to talk to each other, without even considering the need for such a thing; and the custom of writing programs as fast as possible without the need for subsequent alteration.

> 66 The faster we write the wrong sort of programs – the harder it is to meet project deadlines, since projects today call for integrated systems – but we have a growing legacy of segregated programs on which we have to build 99

36% OF IT DIRECTORS ARE APPOINTED BECAUSE THE COMPUTER SYSTEMS CANNOT RESPOND TO THE COMPANY'S NEEDS.

Section 3
Conflicting attitudes of technicians and users

❝Technical people are prima donnas. They don't see the business comes first❞

❝I started off by being evangelical about IT. But it's no good, the users just don't see it. When they talk strategy, they talk production, marketing, maybe finance. Then they'll discuss IT – as a support. IT is secondary. By mere order in the conversation, it's secondary❞

❝ It is not the size of the IT department that is significant. It is its influence. These can be the people that decide the information technology we shall use, the way we shall use it and, ultimately, what capability the company will have to do business ❞

Case

Nothing could have been put over more strongly during the survey interviews with IT directors, which form the basis for this book, than their views on the problems created by the divergent attitudes held by the two key groups involved in the IT revolution: those who use IT, and those who make it work.

For starters, it's a pity that there had to be two groups; that those who use IT couldn't make it work for themselves. But getting the right hardware, and writing the software, was far too technical, far too remote from the training and experience that fitted the users for their job of running the business. And, in the early days, there was no developed computer services industry they could farm it out to – even today it is highly controversial whether operating and programming the machine should be done in-house or contracted out.

It was an inevitable side effect of installing a computer therefore, that a sizeable and, unfortunately, fast-breeding band of technicians was installed alongside it. The 1990 world average was 25 systems development staff employed in a centralised IT department. In the larger companies, the figure can run into several hundreds. But numbers are not its most relevant feature.

The human resources department of a European public utility analysed and contrasted the characteristics of the two groups: the users, and the IT professionals. Each group perceived the other as 'foreigners'.

In the case of the IT specialists, they were foreign to the business –

in the sense that they constituted a relatively new department, whose work was not obviously part of the organization the way that, say, customer sales and service was. Although the department was 28 years old, its staff were perceived as people brought in from outside, who practiced a mysterious trade and spoke a new and incomprehensible jargon. Their trade and jargon was no more difficult for the layman to pick up than that of the engineering department. But the engineers were respected, deferred to; they were the business, they had designed the works, and made the operation possible. Their jargon was one to be proud of. IT jargon was a foreign language and marked the IT specialists as 'not of our community'. The users' perception of the computer went through two distinct phases. At first it was seen as a giant piece of office machinery, something to process the accounts faster but in no way revolutionary. Later, when the computer began to undertake procedures that they themselves used to do, they anthropomorphized it. It was feared as a 'super brain', that would eventually take over their jobs. They began to blame the machine for all their own shortcomings. They were also in some awe of the computer specialists, who received high wages, and who, they could see from reading press advertisements, were in high demand and therefore 'respected'.

The IT specialists also considered the users to be foreigners, in the sense that they were not part of the elite who understood and worked with computers, and to whom the future belonged. The users, they felt, needed to be 'brought up to date'. IT staff were a highly motivated group, excited by the challenge of their work. There were two qualifications to this high motivation however. Their motivation was towards meeting technical objectives, towards making the computer 'stand on its head', rather than towards business objectives. In this regard, they displayed more loyalty to the 'invisible university' of the computer profession than to their employers. This independent attitude was justified since experienced programmers were in short supply and could usually leave and join another firm at an increased salary. 'Getting on' meant getting more valuable computer experience rather than moving up the management hierarchy. This also favoured frequent job changes, since one employer could not provide the latest hardware and variety of applications that furthered their professional careers. Staff turnover was commonly 25% each year in the 70s and early 80s. The second motivational qualification was connected with their work style. They normally worked on projects, which provide the challenge of striving for a clear but temporary objective. It was like the enthusiasm engendered by working on the end-of-term play, which was only performed once, and which contrasted sharply with the sameness of everyday school lessons that were more akin to the work the users do. It was noticeable how morale tapered after projects went live, and how much maintaining programs, once they were written, was disliked, and was often the cause of staff leaving.

Other key differences were found in environmental perspectives. IT professionals generally took a much broader view of the business and were concerned with the overall system, whereas the users were much narrower in outlook, frequently unconcerned and unknowing of what went on outside their department, and felt such prying would be more frowned on than approved by their superiors. Despite this breadth of vision, IT staff were more introverted than the users. They preferred dealing with the mechanics of systems and displayed impatience with the quirks, frailties, intuition and occasional inspiration of its human components.

Altogether, the study reveals a potentially highly negative situation, and goes a long way to explain the we/they attitude which has been blamed for many computer system failures and inadequacies.

It is, however, typical of the attitudes of all alien groups and the communities within which they live. What finally ensures integration is inter-marriage.

As far as the IT alien group is concerned however, there have been very few cases where their members join the user departments, and vice versa. Why is this? Firstly, it seems, we have (for good reasons of shared cost) centralised our technicians, and thus physically separated them from the decentralised users, who are where the action is. The only shared ground is frequently the canteen, but here a 'separate tables' convention is usually found.

Secondly, there has been remarkably little desire for cross-fertilization. IT technicians have not been impressed by offers of career progression by moving into the user areas. Their ambitions and interests lie in IT – which means staying in the IT department, or leaving the company. And the users have found the technical requirement a daunting barrier, and not necessarily in their interests to overcome.

There are some encouraging signs. More and more users are beginning to recognize the benefits of IT, because they are receiving them. And there are more business oriented IT executives who are prepared to take a pragmatic approach.

However, the most important sign is the shift away from the dominance of the central IT department, and the increase in the decentralized use and control of IT. This swing to decentralization is the third of the major trends which have gathered momentum since Watershed in 1985.

IT price reductions have been the spur – putting microcomputers,

> 66 We want to get IT skills into the business. There's a willingness to do it – but it's difficult to orchestrate. What user wants someone with an IT background? On the other hand, someone interested in general management doesn't see two years in systems as being in his interests. There's a feeling of being pushed to the sidelines. After two years, will he be a better man for it, or will he have lost two years in the promotion stakes? 99

> 66 If you can give someone what they really want, what they really have a use for, they're on your side straightaway. This is for us, they say, not a glorification of IT 99

for example, well within the purse limits of departmental managers. The enabler, as we saw in the previous section, has been the deskilling of some programming, and the use of ready-to-use packages.

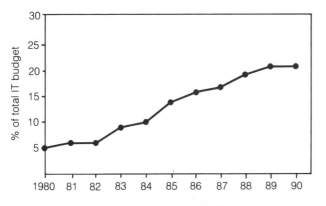

Figure 2.3   User spend as a proportion of total IT budget

The decentralization trend has been a major contributor to today's main problem of segregated systems. It has not stirred up an entirely ill wind. Through involvement, the best training there is, users have acquired some knowledge, lost some apprehensions and gained more positive IT attitudes.

Decentralization has also forced some useful 'bridging' appointments. For example, user responsible business analysts, transporting requirements specifications across the great divide; analyst/programmers, a special hybridized technician who can talk to both humans and computers, reporting to the IT department but especially useful for operating in enemy territory; and IT project managers appointed from the user department.

Despite improved user/technician relations, five fundamental attitude problems remain.

Case

1) *Many of our best technicians are trapped in a time warp*
   An engineering firm in the US was involved in the task of rewriting all their systems to take advantage of the latest server/workstation technology, which was to replace the existing mainframe architecture, and its segregated approach to applications. The IT executive stated that, although the costs and effort required were high, his main problems were the entrenched attitudes of his staff and the users. 'We have many fine analysts and programmers. But the best of them, the most experienced, were brought up on mainframes processing segregated applications. They've become isolated. Look at our typists – they don't sit at typewriters, they sit at computers. The IT guy says 'that's not me, that's wordprocessing.'

But what she types goes into the network. Fax, phones: you can't separate communications from computers anymore. Nor robots. Nor process control. Our IT staff haven't accepted this – haven't taken it on board. Now when we say 'You don't program applications anymore, that's for the users to do. Your job is to design the enabling infrastructure and run it on a server' – it's a whole new concept, and one they're not happy with. Their particular specialism is dying, the worst thing that can happen to a specialist. Also they don't see it as in their interests to have these user initiatives working too successfully. They lose their sphere of influence . . . .'

2) *The users feel information is owned by the department which receives or originates it*
'The users, on the other hand, are happy to run their own applications on local workstations. They have responsibility for results – and they want control over the systems that these results depend on. Where they're not happy is for their information records to be held here, on a centrally maintained database. With corporate access. This gives us the possibility to balance the company's stock levels as a whole. But it takes away some of the local autonomy . . . .'

3) *There is little user understanding of the engineering approach needed to analyse and build computer systems*
'Our main problem is getting user understanding of the time, cost and effort that has to go into building these large IT infrastructures. It's amazing that, in an engineering firm like ours, management are still deeply suspicious of technology. They separate management from the technology of management. It's absurd, like separating a carpenter from his toolbox. But they have very little idea of what computer systems are, or what they do. They have no model of an engineering approach to designing computer systems. Most of them seem to think that changing a computer system is a matter of shouting at it. 'It speaks COBOL doesn't it?' We use anthropomorphic terms like 'language', intelligence' and 'memory', and we've given the user an anthropomorphic model of the computer. The fact that systems design and maintenance is a laborious, engineering process, and is a matter of very, very careful, disciplined control of a complex, engineered product, is something I've so far failed to get through to my users . . . .'

4) *There are a large number of technicians whose motivation is IT excellence, not business excellence*

'Whether it's frustration, despair of user understanding, or a natural tendency we all have to pursue what interests us, and neglect what doesn't, the IT staff will work for weeks, and all night if necessary, to make some obscure routine work 10 milliseconds faster. The fact that it is obscure, and probably wouldn't affect the business if it didn't work at all, seems to escape their deliberations . . . .'

5) *The users, especially top management and the board, don't trust the technicians*
'Maybe we've brought it on ourselves. But you don't get far as a technologist, introducing IT into the business'

We end this section by quoting a remark by one IT director who saw his role very much in terms of unifying user and technician.

'I am a bridge,' he said. 'I have to understand the business plan, and get users to see where IT can help. I have to understand the complexity of computer system architectures, and get the IT specialists to build the right framework to support the business plan.'

One might add, a bridge over much troubled waters. He is, however, not alone.

54% OF IT DIRECTORS STATED ONE OF THEIR SPECIFIC REMITS ON APPOINTMENT WAS TO DEMYSTIFY THE IT DEPARTMENT AND INTEGRATE IT WITH THE REST OF THE COMPANY.

Section 4
Computers for competitive edge

❝It was an accident. We put in the computer system to speed up the accounting procedures – mainly for chasing premium payments. A side-effect was we could pay out small, undisputed claims almost instantly. The marketing boys were onto it straightaway. We captured 40% of the travel insurance business that year!❞

❝There's no such thing as competitive systems – only systems which are used competitively❞

❝ If you're satisfied that you've pared it to the bone, it's providing an efficient service, and isn't spending a dollar more than is needed to maintain that efficiency, then you've cracked the vexed question of 'value for money'. You've got to have an administration, but you're not indulging it! ❞

❝ We tried to justify our computer expenditure on savings – the salaries of the admin. clerks we aimed to replace. It was never quite enough. But we all had this intuition that

Another thing that happened. Not directly as a result of Watershed. The most direct effect of 1985 was the crackdown on computer costs. But, once management got a handle on the IT budget escalation, once the question 'how can we curb runaway spend?' was answered, a new question arose: 'How much should we spend?'

This turned out to be a very complicated question to answer.

The computer had started life in the administration area of the company – automating the payroll, the accounts, the processing of customer orders, updating stock and customer records and so on. How much should be spent on administration? Answer: as little as possible. No more than we need to support the company in its purpose of making and selling goods.

This simple view works fine until we realise that, out of the administration function, comes the information that we need to run the company – to do the all-important making and selling. And with better information, we can make and sell better. And information technology is devoted to providing better information. So, shouldn't we buy more of it?

Yes?

Well, how much more? It's no good saying as much as the information is worth, because no one will put a price on it.

The 'value for money' precept, which management have traditionally used to guide their investment decisions, suddenly doesn't work anymore. Fortunately, a new and unforeseen use for computers appeared, which promised to alleviate the difficulty.

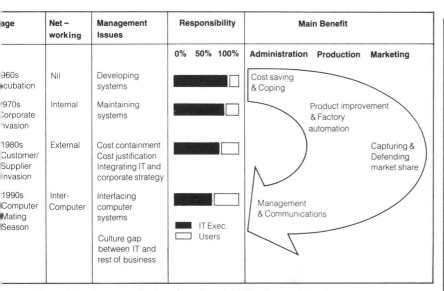

age	Net–working	Management Issues	Responsibility			Main Benefit		
			0%	50%	100%	Administration	Production	Marketing
1960s Incubation	Nil	Developing systems				Cost saving & Coping		
1970s Corporate Invasion	Internal	Maintaining systems					Product improvement & Factory automation	
1980s Customer/ Supplier Invasion	External	Cost containment Cost justification Integrating IT and corporate strategy						Capturing & Defending market share
1990s Computer Mating Season	Inter-Computer	Interfacing computer systems Culture gap between IT and rest of business				Management & Communications		

■ IT Exec. ☐ Users

Figure 2.4   A communications-based model of business computing

Used imaginatively, we were told, IT can provide a competitive edge, it can increase market share. It was the Harvard Business School that told us most eloquently. Thanks to Professor Michael Porter's excellent missionary work, the story of American Airlines acquiring business by securing prime position on the 'flights and prices' booking office display terminals, and of the American Hospital Supply company giving buyers a special terminal, and becoming preferred suppliers by linking them to their computer stock display and ordering system, have set standards for the rest of us to aim at.

Doubtless these well-publicised cases helped to open management's eyes to the new possibilities. Doubtless the post '85 business-oriented IT executive was ready to pick them up.

But the main credit, for what became a swing away from the backshop where it all began, and the acquiring of a new sense of direction by the computer, increasingly aimed at the front shop of the company, increasingly put in direct touch with customer and supplier – the main reason for this trend had to be the technical advances in the communications area of IT.

In fact, the history of business computing can be described as occupying four phases, each neatly fitting a decade, and each determined by the current 'state of the art' in the field of communications. This is illustrated in Figure 2.4.

In the '60s, there were no computer communications. The computer was isolated in a glass cage in head office, where it could be shown off, but not touched. The main objective was saving clerks. The main problem was making it work (the 'meeting project deadlines' issue).

we should go ahead – not just the techies, top management were for the information revolution too. But they wanted to be convinced. The trouble is, you can't put a value on information. On its own, it's worthless. Its only value is the use people make of it **99**

In the '70s it broke out from its incubator, and stretched its tentacles onto the desks of the users, who began feeding it data and interrogating its records for themselves. The main objective was still saving clerks. Since they couldn't put a value tag on the improved information now clearly available, the executive information system protagonists were shy about their objective, and labelled it an 'intangible benefit'. The main problem was still 'meeting project deadlines'. But it was made worse by having to change all the 1960s programs to cope with putting the users in touch with the machine. 'Program maintenance' was added to the IT executive's worry list.

In the '80s, the tentacles stretched even further, and touched the desks of the company's customers and suppliers. The objectives were capturing or defending market share. How could they be otherwise?

In the '90s, as communications increasingly put computers in touch with each other, we can confidently predict much of the benefits will swing back to the administration area, where it all began.

And so we come to the last of the four major IT management trends to emerge in the aftermath of 1985. Figure 2.5 below shows the changing shape of the average computer's applications portfolio.

> 66 We saw our main competitor connect their customers directly with their database. Lights flashed on for us. Once the computer is connected to the market, it must influence the market. We had to follow suit 99

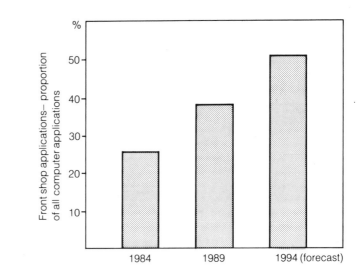

Figure 2.5 Front shop and back shop applications

This survey was carried out in 1988. It shows a sharp rise in the proportion of applications in the production and marketing areas during the period 1983 to 1988, with a prediction that applications for capturing or defending market share could actually outnumber administration applications by 1993.

The main problem in the '80s became 'integrating IT and corporate objectives'. Figure 2.6 below illustrates the drama, as 'meeting project deadlines' is overtaken, after being top of the probs. for
seven years.

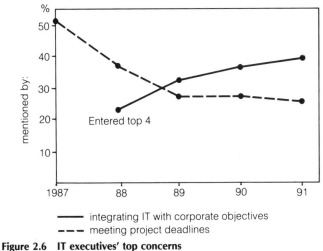

integrating IT with corporate objectives
--- meeting project deadlines

Figure 2.6 IT executives' top concerns

At first sight, it would seem that the opportunity to contribute to
business results, rather than remain as an unavoidable addition to the
overheads, would be welcomed by IT executives. But the problem of
making the computer work was overtaken in 1988 by the problem of
making it work for the company.

Well, we got our priorities right at last. But why was it such a
problem?

A European company in the construction industry responded to
the publicised cases of gaining competitive edge through IT, by
asking its IT department why they had not achieved success in this
area. The IT executive was not involved in the corporate planning
activity, nor in setting corporate objectives. His role was to provide
an efficient data processing service for the company, and he felt
understandably frustrated by the implied criticism. He responded,
in turn, by arranging an internal seminar for the board, at which the
IT department presented, and analysed, all the 'competitive edge'
examples they could find – hoping thereby to stimulate ideas from
the board for similar applications. They found 14 examples. Two
were IT-based methods for improving the product or service – a fast
compilation method for dictionaries of all types, holding a database
of words classified by use etc.; and the dramatic reduction of 'out of
service' time by installing 'in situ' fault diagnosis equipment connected
directly to a central computer. The remaining twelve were all examples
of attracting, and then 'tying-in', either customers or suppliers by

Case

providing them with some unique IT facility. The board felt an insight had been gained from the seminar, and gave the IT department a remit to investigate ways of tying-in their customers or suppliers.

The exercise proved fruitless. The IT executive said later 'We wasted 15 months on the task. Setting out to pioneer the use of a "competitive edge" IT application, means having an idea for a business coup in the first place. Such inspiration is rarely given to the business function executives. For me, in a support role, and with only IT experience, I didn't have the glimmerings of an idea. There must have been others floundering like me, though. I counted eight methodologies for getting competitive edge, offered in books, or at seminars, that year. Why there should be a method for capturing market share for IT, and for no other area of the business, is hard to understand. What we did discover however, was that the insight we felt we'd gained at the board seminar was not the key. The two really important insights, we'd missed completely'.

These two insights were:

1) *Accidental development*
    None of the IT competitive edge cases that the company had examined, had started out with 'gaining competitive edge' as its objective. The systems had, in all cases, been initiated (often by the IT department) as a means of improving administration efficiency. When they were installed, or a very considerable way down the line, a vision of how the system might be used to gain market share had then occurred. This vision always occurred to the line management, never to the IT department.

2) *Non-competitive edge*
    The company found a few examples of pioneers gaining competitive edge. They only gained a short-term lead however. If the IT system brought a significant advantage, it would be imitated – possibly improved on – by their competitors. They concluded, therefore, that what these pioneers were doing was developing a new way of doing business. By following suit, the rest were using IT to defend themselves, to get a place in the new business culture. Rather than gain competitive edge by locking in customers and suppliers, most companies were seeking a non-competitive edge, by forming IT clubs, and locking out those firms who hadn't subscribed to the new system.

66 The bank doesn't plan. Not in the IT sense. A plan to them is go or no go. And if it's go, it's this month 99

The first reason, therefore, why 'front shop' IT causes a problem is that it is hard to find winning applications.

A second reason, particularly related to the way the problem has been expressed (integrating IT with corporate objectives), is the short business horizon mentioned in section 2, compared to the length of time it takes to make things happen in IT.

The third, and most important, reason for the new top IT concern is that, contrary to expectations, the fashionable front shop applications didn't solve the 'How much should we spend?' question. Because, the pay-off couldn't be assessed.

The following were the feelings of one chief executive on the subject: 'You can't count jobs saved anymore. Today, IT's about capturing and defending market share. But how do you measure benefits in this area, to the point where you can say how much you should be spending? I feel I'm being blackmailed most of the time. Not by the suppliers – I expect that. But by my own staff, who never stop telling me what the competition are spending!'

Despite the glamour of this fourth trend – to competitive edge computer applications – few boards appear concerned to exploit the possibility as a deliberate, pioneering initiative.

If it happens, OK. But meanwhile, they are much more concerned about value for money – from IT in general, but particularly from front shop applications.

> ONLY 4% OF IT DIRECTORS SAID THEY HAD BEEN APPOINTED TO EXPLOIT THE POSSIBILITY OF THE COMPUTER TO CAPTURE MARKET SHARE.

66 Few companies can point to applications for capturing market share. Most of us use IT to defend ourselves by jumping on technological bandwagons, and then worrying about justifying this IT spend on defence 99

Section 5
The novelty of IT

❝ Those who run the business have enormous difficulty accepting that IT is a part of the business strategy. For centuries, business has been about making things, marketing things, and managing money. Businessmen have done their job and earned their living by being expert in one or more of these areas. To consider anything else as being of equal or possibly of greater importance is a very new idea ❞

❝ I started off being evangelical about IT. Then I spent seven years wondering why I couldn't persuade others to the view I hold. You can't teach it. They have to discover the truth for themselves ❞

❝ The engineer was king in the first stage of the industrial revolution. The information systems engineer should be king now. But until we stop saying 'We must have information', and people with vision say why, and what use that information is, IT will not be respected ❞

❝ Most technologies leverage muscular activity. Information technology leverages mental activity ❞

We are living in the second stage of the industrial revolution. Because we are living in it, it can be hard for us to see what is actually happening.

What happened in the first stage is clear enough. Machines were invented, which enormously extended the physical power of human beings to do things. It was revolutionary because it extended mankind's ability to produce in quantity, to move at speed and to reshape the environment.

In this, the second stage, machines are extending the power of human beings to control.

This stage heralds an even more profound revolution. By the middle of the twentieth century, the first stage had virtually come to an end, further progress being constrained by man's inability to control machines of greater sophistication, since they worked faster than he could think.

He was also unable to control effectively organizations of the greater size and complexity needed to sustain progress.

Most important, he could no longer rely on the supply of an obedient workforce.

The second stage is more profound because it overcomes these constraints on further progress. In doing so, it challenges the role of human beings more fundamentally than did the first stage — which only removed the burden of hard work; a burden most were glad to relinquish.

The second stage of the industrial revolution promises to remove the burden of control. And removing the burden of control is so close to losing control that the prospect is both exciting and frightening.

No matter where they've come from — enthusiastic technician or converted user, a tough administrator press-ganged into the job or a visionary who volunteers for it — sooner or later everyone who manages IT experiences the same frustration. They gain an insight into the real nature of the information technology revolution which they are unable to share with their colleagues in the rest of the company.

This failure, not so much of communication — the computer age is rammed down our throats until we are numb to the phrase — but of any real perception of IT's potential by those who fashion our destiny, and that of the world, is the major cause, both of IT management's frustration in attempting to integrate computers with corporate plans, and of general management's disappointment over the return on IT investment.

A number of large companies, subscribers to a satellite broadcasting company, were so concerned over the failure of users and general management to appreciate the fundamental nature of the information revolution that they commissioned a special introductory training program. The broadcast script was as follows:
'We are told a revolution is going on. An information revolution. We've heard tell about the industrial revolution. About how James Watt watched his kettle boil, and instead of making the tea like millions before him, he went right outside and invented the steam engine. Which pumped water, powered tractors, pulled trucks and carriages full of goods and people and, in broad terms, put the horse out of business. The effect of using machines to supplement or replace human and animal muscle has undoubtedly been revolutionary.'

66 IT was a black box five years ago. Everyone was keen to learn. Now, they don't see it as a problem, just an enabling technology extending the office printer, the adding machine, the filing system and the telephone. But there are fundamental management issues which they must own **99**

Case

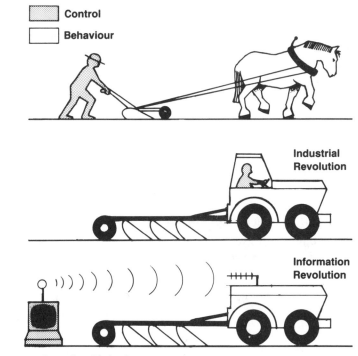

Figure 2.7   Control and behaviour

'The industrial revolution was about doing things – quicker, better, abundantly; things previously impossible. The information revolution is about controlling things – quicker, better, over greater distances and in ways previously impossible. It is the invention of the computer that has enabled the information revolution to get under way. Things which previously human beings had to see for themselves, work out for themselves and communicate for themselves can now be done by machines. This revolutionises control in three important ways.'
'The first way is to provide, not just information, but knowledge. The computer provides knowledge firstly by storing large quantities of data in its memory or database. How it remembers data is unimportant. The current technology records it as magnetised spots on spinning discs – but the techniques have changed and will change many times more. This data is turned into information by associating it with other items of data – so that if you mention a particular customer the computer will tell you what colour socks he last bought – if you say "red socks", it will tell you all the customers with that particular penchant. The database holds data and associations. It holds far more data than the human brain. The point is made, when we acknowledge that a computer can easily remember the telephone numbers, the names and the addresses of everyone in the world. It has to gather the data first, which can be a problem. But once stored it never forgets, and can recall it quickly and with perfect accuracy. This is one way it adds to its

user's knowledge – the volume of information it can provide, and the speed and accuracy of recall. Where human memory scores is in the richness of associations we can remember. We may not be acquainted with all the people in the world. But the intimate details we remember about the few that we do know extends to very much more than the colour of their socks.'

'The other way the computer adds to knowledge is the way it can work out possibilities and probabilities. We all do this when we control our behaviour or that of others and of machines. Before turning the steering wheel, or instructing our chauffeur to do so, we anticipate the effect. Before marketing a new product, we anticipate the market's reaction. We are very good at this when we've been down similar paths before, and things behave much as they did before. We call people armed with this knowledge "experienced", and we pay a lot for them. But we are very bad at it when we break new ground, or things start behaving unpredictably. We use "trial and error", which is slow. The computer however is very fast at this trial and error game. It is also tireless, maintains complete accuracy each time round and can consider large numbers of factors which affect the situation, whereas humans usually boggle if they have to think about more than two or three things going on at the same time. This is another way the computer can add to knowledge – it can work out possible courses of action and likelihoods of success.'

'We have talked about how information technology can bring about a revolution in the sphere of control by adding to knowledge. Be clear – man still controls in this case. He decides what he should do, tells others what to do or instructs machines – but he does this with the benefit of knowledge supplied by a machine. This enables him to control things better, or, for example in the case of high speed aircraft, to control things otherwise beyond his ability.'

'Many people concentrate on the provision of more knowledge as the key to the information revolution. In doing so, they miss two other vital ways that computers affect our lives. The second way information technology revolutionizes control is to allow machines to do the controlling themselves. This is called automation. Before the computer was invented there were examples of automation. In the sixteenth century windmills were turning themselves into the wind, and adjusting their sails to allow for the strength of the wind. Lavatory cisterns were a later benefit for mankind, but when they arrived, they refilled themselves with water automatically by virtue of a floating arm which operated the inlet valve. But these were tailormade control machines, designed to control one specific activity. The computer's distinction is that it is a general-purpose control machine. If the rules for controlling a situation are known, and are then provided in a "program", a computer can handle it. Computers can control machines: there are computers embedded in washing machines checking the water temperature, the time and what stage of the wash it's at – and they can control human beings: checking a customer's credit limit and the amount he already owes and then instructing a salesman whether to proceed with the sale. Computers are better at control than human beings where the rules governing the situation are known – but not where discretion is required. Think about this for a moment.'

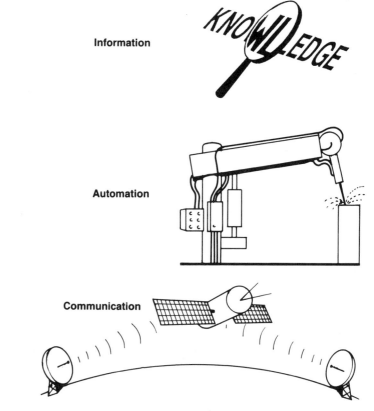

Figure 2.8   The impact of information technology

'It's rather like the distinction between reflex and discretionary control in animals. Where the rules are known, for example for digesting food, standing upright on only two legs or maintaining body temperature, animals derive considerable benefit in delegating control to their reflexes. The reflexes are quick, what to do doesn't have to be thought out afresh each time and, most important, reflex control frees up the animal to concentrate on something else which requires all its attention. Reflexes provide automatic control systems in single organisms. A major result of the information revolution is that the computer is enabling us to build reflex control systems for organisations. What are the advantages of reflex control? In addition to speed and to freeing-up people to concentrate on discretionary control, which is where our abilities and job satisfactions really lie, we can add benefits like accuracy, tirelessness, consistency, and not suffering from boredom. And we can add obedience. This last is the key to the revolution. Human beings are wilful. Computers obey their programs. What is it worth to secure unquestioning obedience?'

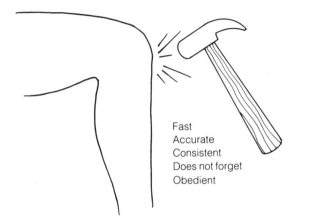

Fast
Accurate
Consistent
Does not forget
Obedient

Figure 2.9   Reflex control

'The third way information technology revolutionizes control is to extend dramatically our power to communicate – both with each other and with machines. Communications are the glue which binds an organization together. Men can combine with each other, and with machines to form organizations. But if one human being cannot communicate with another within an allowable timespan, they cannot, in any practical sense, be considered members of the same organization. Similarly, if we cannot communicate with a particular machine, it cannot co-operate with us. By extending our power to communicate, information technology has revolutionized the concept of organization. The size and influence of an organization was previously constrained by the distance, the number and the sensory perceptions (vision and hearing, etc.) of its members. Through the communication networks provided by information technology these constraints are rapidly being removed.'

'In summary, the industrial revolution was about using machines to help us make things; the information revolution is about using machines to help us control things. The industrial revolution had got stuck. Further progress meant building machines and organizations we could no longer control. The information revolution is removing these constraints.'

It seems simple enough: more knowledge to hand, automation where the rules for control are known, and greatly extended communication. But when it's not just in a few, but in every company in the world, that a substantial number of people fail to grasp the significance of IT – the point is made that new perceptions about how the world could work are only slowly and painfully acquired.

Most organizations go through four distinct stages of perception regarding the computer:

Case

A major European financial institution held a seminar for its IT staff, to discuss the implications of recent technological changes on system design. In his introduction to the seminar, the IT manager, who had spent the last 25 years of his career managing the computer department, highlighted the major attitudes changes of the user managers which the company had experienced in that time.

Stage I – *Excitement*
'Before the first computer was purchased, and for the first four years of its life, top management was enthusiastic. For some time it had been getting harder and harder to recruit able, educated people who were prepared to do routine clerical tasks. The business was also getting more complicated, and it was difficult to get reliable information on how things were going. They believed the machine would save clerks – and be a ready-made mine of information. Our main job, as computer experts at that time, was to restrain them from eagerly signing hardware cheques on the mere say-so of a computer manufacturer.'

Stage II – *Addition to the overheads*
'But we did not save the clerks we'd hoped to. And the machine was not a mine of information, and was extremely difficult and unfriendly to use. The costs escalated and programming took for ever. The company became disenchanted and our department got criticised as an "unwelcome addition to the overheads".'

Stage III – *Competitive edge*
'During the '80s, two major technological changes brought the users back in favour of IT. Improved communications and cheap hardware meant computers could be decentralized and the users could begin to do their own thing. They plunged with renewed enthusiasm into simple, ad hoc systems and packages which yielded short-term benefits. This idea that the computer could be a profit earner, and not just a cost centre, was reinforced by some attractive publicity given to a number of companies claiming to have achieved competitive edge through the imaginative use of IT. Nearly all the cases cited were examples of companies making use of the improved communications facilities, and "tying-in" their customers or suppliers by connecting

them to their computer in some way. Pressure to identify so-called strategic uses for computers, with quick payback, spread to most installations.'

Stage IV – *Infrastructures*
'A number of companies are now recognizing that survival rather than competitive edge is the reason for IT investment, and are rejecting "short termism" as anything more valuable than a strategy for educating and enthusing users and the Board. What is fundamental to this new attitude is the recognition of the need to lay down IT infrastructures – databases, communications, and the high volume processing jobs – the "core" systems which have no direct benefit, but which provide the framework on which the applications for the next ten years will be hung.'

It seems we still have to wait for a fifth stage, in which mankind will perceive the nature of the changes that IT can bring about. The novelty of IT is the one really fundamental problem about managing it.

It seems to be a problem of extremes. On the one hand, the computer is perceived as a mystery, we are in awe of it and, deep down, most of us reject it, it is not something for us.

Information, on the other hand, is an all too familiar and boring word. It suggests to us what we read in the newspapers, hear on the radio or learn from books. And, if all the information revolution means is that we are going to have to look at computer screens for much of this stuff, well, what's so revolutionary about that?

What are the insights about the information revolution that the computer-weathered develop, yet find so hard to pass on? There seem to be three of them:

1 *There are three components of IT*
In addition to storing and retrieving information, which is commonly thought to be all that the information revolution is about (and justified by the doubtful belief that management would benefit if it had more information), Information Technology affords the possibility of:

● automatically manipulating that information
● automatically controlling all the routine processes in the world
● connecting all mankind and all machines together in instant communication networks.

2 *Information is the key resource in any organization*
In contrast with the common view that the key functions in any business are making and selling its goods or services, both Production

❝ It is the Operating Information System, not the Management Information System, that is causing the revolution **❞**

❝ When we dream, when we read a book,

❝we can accept, for those moments, that information becomes reality. But when we wake, when we put down our book, we do no more than substitute one information source for another. As managers, we need not debate whether there is a reality beyond the information layer, for we cannot approach it closer. All we can do, in managing and manipulating the world, is to receive, to record, to process and to transmit information **❞**

❝Yesterday, IT was about managing experts. Today, it is the very stuff of management. Tomorrow, it may be the only thing that needs to be managed **❞**

and Marketing are suddenly seen to be no more than the management of information – information about customers, the marketplace, resources, possibilities; manipulating that information; and the issuing of messages and instructions to people and machines.

3 *Computers release rather than replace people*
The hope of some, and the fear of many, that computers will replace people is seen to be misplaced. Activity is seen to consist of two types: what might be called 'structured' activity, where the rules for performing it are known; and 'unstructured' activity, where they aren't. All the structured activity, in marketing, production and in administration, will be performed by machines. This, plus answers at our fingertips and the immensely expanded communication powers afforded by IT, will take the brakes off further growth. Growth for an organization, however, will mean bigger markets, and increasing the integration of the 'raw materials to goods-in-the-hand' production and distribution chain. It will no longer mean more people. The slave class of factory and office workers will disappear as their work is performed by computers. Many people will work in small businesses, providing the personal touch missed by mass-production; and through agencies, or sometimes on their own, as subcontractors satisfying the fluctuating needs of the large organizations for special skills.

But IT is still too new for these insights to have become generally accepted. The thirty years that we have been using computers is nothing when it comes to a fundamental change of perceptions; especially when most of those years have been about doing it wrong, and living with user and top management disappointment.

> THE 'CULTURE GAP' BETWEEN THOSE KNOWLEDGEABLE ABOUT IT AND COMPANY MANAGERS AND USERS IN GENERAL IS STATED BY 62% OF IT DIRECTORS TO BE THEIR TOP PROBLEM.

Section 6
The board's view

❝We've had this worry for so long. Let's get a man in!❞

❝They don't know. But if they know a man who does, they're happy with that❞

❝They want someone they can trust. Trouble is, they trust fellow businessmen. They know how to assess businessmen❞

❝To get the question 'why?' taken seriously – even to get it asked at all – you have to be on the board. When it comes to IT strategy, no one at that level is going to embarrass themselves by asking the stupid question. And ranting on about how vital it all is, from a seat in front of the computer control panel – that just makes it worse. If you want real conversation to take place, you have to be one of them❞

'We've had this worry for so long!' What worry? What is it about IT that gives the boards of the world's largest companies such cause for concern?

Well, the original concern was cost. There is no question about that. The size of the IT investment, and the seemingly uncontrollable cost escalation that we discussed in section 1, turned the board's original enthusiasm for computers into disenchantment, and then into serious anxiety.

But, as we also saw in section 1, this anxiety eventually led to the ending of any fear of the technocrats who drew up each year's exciting IT budget, and an ending of any respect for their business judgement.

We have termed 1985 as the 'watershed year' for computers. In that year, they retained their mystery, but they lost their magic. Proposals for fresh investment had to pass the 'measurable business benefit' test. Budgets for keeping the existing computer ship afloat were scrutinised for any means of cost reduction or containment. As a result, the world's spend by the centralised IT departments was held in check.

> BY 1987, 77% OF CHIEF EXECUTIVES STATED THEY WERE
> 'SATISFIED' OR 'FAIRLY SATISFIED' WITH THE EFFICIENCY OF
> THEIR COMPUTER DEPARTMENTS.
>
> ONLY 8% FELT THERE WAS ROOM FOR ANY FURTHER
> SIGNIFICANT COST REDUCTION.

There were two important side-effects of the IT spend cutback attempts.

Firstly, many companies have complained that, for a number of years, IT stood still. Secondly, the image of the IT executive changed. In no time at all, he had to cultivate a talent for watching dollars rather than IBM.

Case

A major Australian bank doubled its IT expenditure between 1981 and 1984. There were no clerical savings to set against the increased investment, and the 1985 budget, which proposed a further 30% growth to cope with a projected increase in the number of transactions to be processed, failed to get board approval. Instead, the board required that a special task force be set up to study and recommend ways of containing costs. Following an eight week study, the task force reported its findings. They contained two main recommendations: to 'shop around' for cheaper equipment instead of following their single supplier policy, and to improve the IT department's efficiency. They identified several areas where efficiency improvements appeared to be feasible. Instead of recommending the measures to take however, they proposed a new management technique. Costs should be related to the computer's output. The IT executive's objectives should be to reduce the cost per unit of output by 10% every six months. The board accepted the recommendation, and further decided to split the IT function, reporting to two general managers, on the grounds that one man should not have so much power over expenditure.

Five years later, a single director was appointed to co-ordinate the IT function. 'The results of the cost containment exercise were spectacular,' he said. 'In real terms, our computer spend didn't increase for four years, at a time when the volume of business more than doubled. But it caused us to miss out on a number of the business opportunities now offered by IT. We just didn't consider doing anything new. All our time and energy was taken up trying to reduce the running and enhancement costs of what we were already doing. Having two general managers didn't help. A co-ordinated plan for the future just wasn't on. And one of them had no IT background or feel for the subject at all. He was an excellent administrator. He was out to cut costs, and he cut them dramatically. Unfortunately, it was a very bad moment to get into a time warp. The face of IT was changing rapidly – but we're still stuck with the old 'COBOL plus giant mainframe' mentality.'

BETWEEN 1987 AND 1989 IN THE UNITED STATES, 36% OF CHIEF INFORMATION OFFICERS – MEN WHOSE CLAIM TO BE TOP IT EXECUTIVE WAS BASED ON TECHNICAL EXPERTISE – WERE EITHER MADE REDUNDANT, OR DOWNGRADED NUMBER TWO TO A COST-CUTTING BOSS.

No one would decry the attention paid to productivity by the new style IT executives. A variety of measurement techniques were introduced in computer departments in the late '80s. A glance at the nature of these techniques shows that the whole thrust of management at that time was to improve the computer's efficiency however; its effectiveness, the extent to which it satisfied the needs of the users, continued to be a neglected area.

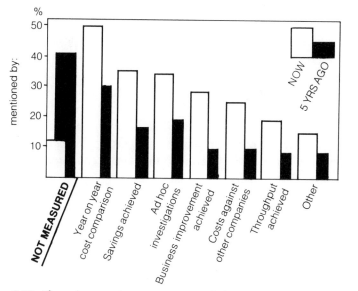

Figure 2.10   The main computer measurement techniques in use

It was perfectly true that most boards were becoming satisfied with the cost containment measures applied, and believed that there was little more to be squeezed out of their existing investment. But their concerns did not stop there. Once the passive mood of accepting the computer expert's advice had been replaced by the active one of challenge, new thinking about IT began to emerge at board level. Five key questions were asked.

- Major advances were being claimed for the latest IT products. How long should the old ship be kept afloat?
- The benefit of productivity gains and deskilling were being claimed for the latest systems development products. Was it still necessary

to rely on a centralized pool of mysterious technocrats to make computers work?

- Would networks and the use of cheaper computers distributed around the organisation mean that the centralized computer overhead could be disbanded?
- Or could the IT management problem be got rid of altogether – by buying in computer time and systems development from the growing computer services industry?
- Above all, was the value-for-money problem as intractable as it appeared? Were we doomed for ever to invest in IT as an act of faith with no earthly reward, or was there something in the stories circulating about using computers to gain competitive edge?

To have achieved cost control was not enough. The board remained uncomfortable with the indeterminate but worrying thought that opportunities were being missed.

Case

66 In the directors' eyes, IT was not performing. They couldn't get at the information they needed; they couldn't recruit skilled people who would deliver; the network was unable to respond to the company's requirements 99

A major engineering firm in the United States was organized in four major divisions, corresponding to the four categories of product they manufactured. Each company was virtually a business in its own right. Nevertheless, they had installed a centralized data processing department which provided computer services to the whole firm. The major complaint of the users was that the computer did little to help with the problem of production control, especially with parts availability, and, in addition, prevented them from chasing and rectifying holdups manually.

Top management were frustrated by their attempts to resolve the difficulties through their IT executive. He had been recruited some twelve years before for his technical abilities. He had never become integrated into the business however, and they felt that discussions about computer systems always foundered on the technical issues of why something had to be or could not be done. They lost faith in his advice, and resolved that the management of computers should be given to someone with a business rather than a computer background, 'One of us,' as they put it. 'Someone who's had responsibility for bottom line results. Above all, someone who speaks our language.' None of the existing members of the executive suite could be released, or wanted to take the job. So they recruited, from outside the firm, a production engineer who had also run his previous company's computer department. Despite his appointment on a level with the divisional directors, the new man soon complained that it would be a slow job to get a real acceptance of the role IT should play in the fortunes of the company. 'In my previous job,' he said, 'it was a small firm. I was the only production director. I had a vision of how IT could help and I went ahead and did it. Here there is enormously more scope. IT will eventually

transform the business. But top management doesn't want to know. They wanted someone to see them through the technical problems they didn't understand. Someone they could trust. Someone with furthering the business rather than installing computery as his main concern. Someone they could rely on not to overspend, but without involving them with computer problems so they could get on with running the business.'
'Now the four divisional vice-presidents here are powerful people. Essentially what they weren't getting, and what they wanted me to provide, were short-term IT solutions to their management information problems to cure the pain of non-available parts. What they didn't want to hear, but what I have had to tell them, is that there aren't any short term solutions; that if IT is going to help smooth out the delivery bottlenecks then a long-term view must be taken of a computer system which co-ordinates the design and scheduling of components, and which cuts back on their divisional autonomy to some extent. Instead of taking IT off their backs, recruiting me has resulted in their having to face more fundamental systems problems than before. They cannot escape being involved in the way computer systems affect the business, just as I cannot escape being involved in the business problems that they have to face. They say they want an IT man to be one of them. What I've just said are the two implications of such an appointment, and they don't like either of them!'

Before 1985, it was rare for the IT executive to be on the board. The cost containment exercise, which took off in that year, was also accomplished without the computer hatchet men reporting directly to the chief executive.

It was the subsequent concern of the board that IT was, in some way, more important than had been thought, that cost cutting, carried too far, might affect survival, that opportunities were being missed and that value for IT money might be reflected in the bottom line, that persuaded them to consider elevating the management of the company's IT investment from departmental to board level.

In a nutshell, the board's view was that computers were becoming too important to be managed by computer people. Such men were dangerous. Their investment proposals were based on technical feasibilities, which not only took the board out of its depth, and inhibited discussion, but were completely secondary to business considerations.

Since the technical possibilities and business improvement potential were not apparent to them, they wished to delegate computer management to someone else. This person should be one of the board to end any 'us and them' atmosphere between the technicians and the users, and, most important, to end for ever the situation that someone outside the board had such power over the company's fortunes.

> 66 You have to ask yourself, What is the main worry in the executive suite – is it economies, is it environmental issues, whatever. If the company is run by pain philosophy, IT will always be overlooked. Because the only pain IT gives you is its cost. Cut it back and it doesn't hurt so much 99

66 Soon after my appointment as IT director, I had this confrontation with one of the other board members. 'It's not your job to tell me about issues that will affect my performance,' he said. He had no perception that I had any responsibility to talk about anything other than the wizardry of technology 99

And, like the rest of the board, they should have a proven business record so that they could be trusted.

But, although the IT director should be a business man, it was not the board's view that he should have any responsibility for business strategy.

ONLY 5% OF IT DIRECTORS HAVE 'DETERMINING THE EFFECT OF IT ON THE FUTURE OF THE BUSINESS' AS ONE OF THEIR MAIN ROLES.

ONLY 4% OF IT DIRECTORS HAVE ANY SPECIFIC RESPON-SIBILITY FOR GETTING BENEFITS FROM THE COMPANY'S INVESTMENT IN IT.

Chapter 3

The IT director's job

66 The importance of IT is not the spend. It is the degree of reliance we place on it. Business today is IT. We'd all fall apart without it. As IT director, my main concern is that we stay alive 99

Section 1
The trend to appoint IT directors

❝The average board have no IT knowledge at all. But if they ignore IT when they make a plan, they're dead. They need someone to protect them❞

❝They said 'IT's your problem now – get on with it.' But since my appointment to the board, I've given them more heartaches than they ever had before❞

❝Building and managing the common IT infrastructure is how I see my role. That's not how the board saw it when I was appointed two and a half years ago. We had separate computer applications then. My brief was to look at spend❞

The board may well have been excited by the thought of their first computer. Indeed, why else would they have purchased it – there was no hard evidence of any benefit in the 60s! But, although intrigued by its potential, there was no thought or intention that its management merited board level attention.

There were some notable, but isolated, examples of IT directors appointed in the 70s. The trend, however, to promote responsibility for the function to board level began in a small way at the beginning of the 80s, some twenty years after computers first started to be used in business.

Figure 3.1 shows that it took off in earnest around 1988, and, by 1992, it is predicted that 68% of companies with computer departments will have an IT executive on the board.

This prediction is based on the expectations of chief executives to make such an appointment; if they haven't done so already. The trend is more marked in the larger companies. The statistics refer to those having responsibility for IT, and specifically for integrating IT with corporate objectives. It is not based on titles, for example that of IT director. Many IT executives hold the title director, vice-president, chief information officer and so on, without being a member of the main board. Conversely, there are some doing the job of an IT director, but with no clue in their title that they are doing so.

IT may be the sole responsibility of the director concerned, or it may be combined with some other function; finance or production for example. The key point, and the criterion for inclusion in these statistics, is that the person proposing IT investments and strategy, and responsible for its cost and operation, is on the main board.

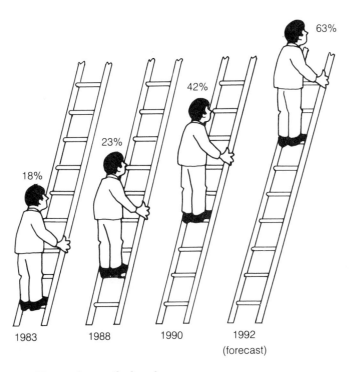

Figure 3.1   IT executives on the board

70% OF THE UK'S TOP 500 COMPANIES HAVE A MAIN BOARD DIRECTOR RESPONSIBLE FOR INTEGRATING IT WITH CORPORATE OBJECTIVES.

The trend is closely connected with the 1985 IT Watershed year, analyzed in chapter 1. Top management's determination to control escalating computer costs, and the success achieved, had one embarrassing side-effect. It raised the question 'How much should we spend?'

The one person they couldn't ask was the old-style, technology-enthused IT executive – since it was his spend that they had sought to curb. The repercussions of the crackdown are illustrated in Figure 3.2

Cost control raised issues of value for money from investing in IT, which no one at board level had ever had to face. Furthermore, if IT can be used to capture or defend market share (a novel idea then beginning to be debated), maybe we should be spending more, not seeking to cut back?

66 The job of the IT executive has always been to save costs. In the early days, the game was to cut back on the firm's people costs. Then somebody noticed that this caused

us to spend a lot on computers. Now we have a new war cry: cut back on computer costs! **99**

Some sought to push the question back onto the users' shoulders. Charging for IT became more popular. These charging systems made the users pay for every use they made of the computer, instead of writing off these costs to the overheads. If the users are prepared to pay, the argument ran, they must be getting value. But others, a small minority at first, appointed someone at board level to sort out these questions. Two years after crackdown, the number of board appointments rose dramatically. After a steady but slow rise in the middle of the decade, in the space of two years, 1989 and 1990, they doubled. It seemed the day of the IT director had arrived.

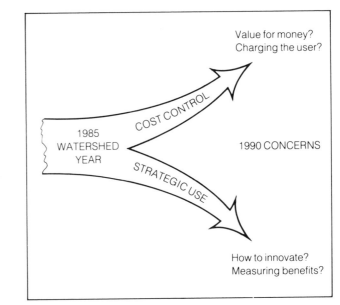

Figure 3.2   Repercussions of crackdown

The reasons for appointing IT directors given by the board were analyzed in the end of the last chapter. They may be summarized as appointing someone they can trust, to:
- Control IT costs
- Overcome IT system delivery bottlenecks
- Remove the feelings of discomfort when questions of IT investment are raised at board level

Whilst accepting that these reasons were why they were appointed, the perception of the IT directors themselves, of what their job really is, are quite different.

Case

A large European paper manufacturer had appointed a succession of people with considerable IT experience to manage their IT investment.

By 1988 they were complaining of excessive costs, and, in the directors' eyes, IT was not performing. They appointed one of their divisional managers, already a regional board director, onto the main board with responsibility for IT. He recounted the reasons for his appointment, as he saw them. 'We were concerned about the high level of IT costs. Not about escalation – we'd cracked that one: a whole host of output measurements now tell us what we're spending and why. There's no more to screw out of efficiency. And justifying new spend is tough; we ask for measured bottom line and that's end of story for most IT dreams. Fortunately, my appointment has coincided with new offerings in the IT field. The cost performance breakthroughs achieved by micros ten years ago, are now available at the mainframe level. By just replacing our mainframes with servers and putting powerful workstations on the users' desks I can make attractive savings in the IT budget. This has given me enormous credibility, since cost reduction possibilities were a key reason for my appointment. It's also true that our previous IT manager might not have made these savings. He was a self-confessed technocrat, and probably wouldn't have been prepared to give so much of his empire to the users. But I don't see this as the main reason for my job. There are three key tasks to be done, and they can only be done by someone on the board.'

'Firstly, we have to free up people to concentrate on the sales function. Automate the routine work, and give them product and customer information on tap. This is quite different from the old objective of replacing people. To achieve it, there has to be a new marketing strategy as well as new IT systems. As a main board director, I'm involved in deciding these strategies.'

> 66 We're not replacing people. We're releasing them 99

'Secondly, we have to identify the commonality in our systems. IT used to be put in where the pain was felt. We developed separate systems for each user. If the IT department had said no, we're going to design a common system, the director concerned would railroad it through, because he'd lose a measure of control. And there's a natural proprietorial attitude to information. Customer records are held in fifteen places for example, and always in a slightly different form. Remember, these guys are powerful directors who have achieved success by ploughing individual furrows vigorously and selfishly. But now we are beginning to lay down common IT infrastructures, because I have the power to take them on.'

> 66 You can't manage a business in slices if you want to meet today's efficiency needs 99

'Thirdly, as a main board director, I'm involved in generating the business plan, not just accepting it as a *fait accompli* and supporting it with IT. This lifts the position of IT to be part of the company. It puts us in the airlines and banking class.'

All IT directors interviewed cited the airlines and the banks as examples of where IT was accepted at board level as being of strategic importance.

> 66 We're not sophisticated enough

66 to set IT director objectives. I set my own. But this will change when the board see IT as a strategic resource 99

66 I couldn't spell out the bottom line. But as a director, I had the opportunity to convince my colleagues to give the idea a chance. I had the power to put my ideas into practice. And I had the responsibility of my job on the line if it failed 99

66 Before accepting, I laid down two conditions. I had to report direct to the chief executive, and I wanted the guarantee of my old job back after three years 99

It was a popular goal to achieve that same level of acceptance for IT in their companies, no matter what business they were in.

A notable fourth reason for positioning IT at Board level was given by just a few. These were the visionaries. People who had a perception of the use of IT to gain competitive edge, and who freely admitted they were taking a business risk in persuading their colleagues to invest in their ideas.

If the board's view can be summed up as 'get this computer problem off our backs and give it to someone we can trust', most IT directors see their job as somehow convincing their top management colleagues of the strategic importance of IT, and then carefully loading it back onto their shoulders. And if that seems to imply that many see their appointment as a short-term expedient – well, initially, many do.

Furthermore, IT, coupled with responsibility for bottom line, is also seen as a hot potato, especially by those without thorough background experience in the area. From a career point of view, a spell in IT looks like a step backwards, and possibly a fatal one.

But after a while, perceptions change, unexpected challenges and insights emerge, and a radical restructuring of traditional management was expressed by some as a possibility, and one which positioned IT on a par with production and marketing as one of the prime factors of business success. However tenuous, the case was argued with conviction.

IT Protagonist: Why is production considered a front line function?

Doubter: It produces the raison d'etre of the business. If we are in raisins, then drying grapes is what it's all about.

P: But drying grapes isn't enough. We've got to sell them to stay in business.

D: Yes – marketing is key too. Production and marketing are the two front line performers.

P: But you can't make raisins without grapes. Buying grapes is just as important as turning them into raisins.

D: No. Purchasing isn't in the front line. It doesn't make or sell the product. That's the point. Everything else is support.

P: You mean if we grew the grapes instead of buying them, getting grapes would become a front line activity?

D: [pause]   Yes.

P: And if we bought some and grew the rest?

D: Look, we're splitting hairs. I'm defining front line activities as making and selling.

P: OK. That's a clear definition. But what's so important about front line activities? Boards have directors responsible for front line activities, and also for support activities — finance, human resources and so on.

D: But they don't have a director responsible for the canteen. To merit a seat on the board, a support function has to be critical to success.

P: Access to company information, systems for handling the daily transactions — an efficient IT infrastructure. This is critical for every sizeable organisation today.

D: [smiling confidently] There are many critical infrastructures: the electricity supply, telephones and so on. But no one is suggesting a director of telephones.

P: Because there isn't much you can do with your telephones. They're either there or they aren't.

[kindly] When you said, 'To be represented on the board, a support function has to be critical to success', I think you meant it has to involve critical choices. So the justification for an IT director can only be that IT is in the front line of the business. That it is the product, or it sells it. Or, if it's what you call a support function, the IT choices involved are critical for survival?

D: Yes, I think that's true. And there are examples. The banks, where the product is information: account balances. And the airlines, where sales depend totally on IT: the screens-based passenger reservation systems.

P: But isn't all marketing about conveying information? And don't all products contain a vital element of IT, either in their finished state or in their production process?

D: You could argue that. Not everyone would agree.

P: [triumphant] Exactly. The only ones who'd agree would be those who had a conviction that IT was vital. And this would vary from industry to industry, and from time to time and according to individual perceptions. Suppose the technology advanced, and drying grapes became child's play. And selling them, provided the quality and price were right, was just order taking. Suppose the whole key to success was buying the right grapes in the first place. The best grapes at the right price. Wouldn't purchasing be a front line role? Wouldn't the buyer merit a place on the board?

D: He certainly would. He might conceivably be the chief executive.

P: Because it would be obvious. By then, everyone would see buying was the key activity. It's what's seen to be important at the time. When IT is perceived as the key activity in business, it will be represented on the board as a matter of course.

D: [now seeing the trap] Many boards feel IT is vital, because they don't understand it. They appoint an IT director out of fear. It's a short-term appointment. As soon as they're comfortable with its concepts and relevance they'll fire him.

P: OK. But that doesn't destroy the argument. While IT is perceived as vital it will merit board representation. It's only a matter of time before all companies, not just banks and airlines, perceive IT as vital.

D: It's an argument.

P: I can think of others.

[he gets up and begins to pace the room]   Most people would agree that hierarchical structures are insufficient. But matrix organisations, which recognise the interaction of line and support functions aren't much better – because the degree of interaction is constantly changing. It's the dynamic organisation that wins today. A fluid structure that's based on project management; that lives till its objectives are achieved, and then reforms as something else. And who is the natural project leader? The IT director. Because his is the only resource that pervades all the others. IT is the basis of all control.

[he warms to his subject]   And what about the company secretary? He often merits a place on the board to protect the company against mistakes in its legal dealings. But the security of a company's IT systems are equally vital. No company can afford to suffer the breakdown or penetration of its computer systems today – we can't manage without them. Shouldn't there be an IT director fulfilling the company secretary's role in this new field? . . .

[he is still talking as the curtain falls]

The most cogent arguments for IT representation at board level came from the chief executive of a European food manufacturer.

Case

The company had listed the three main objections to an IT director. They were:

- IT is not in the front line.
- IT is not the business. It can only support the business.
- The makers and the sellers are key to the business. All other functions are in a subsidiary position.

66 In future, the only way companies will compete will be through better software 99

The chief executive took each of the objections in turn. 'As to the first – IT is not in the front line – the concept of line and staff functions traditionally comes from the military. The infantry divisions fought the war, they were the line; the signals corps, services corps and medical corps supported the infantry with information, weapons and treatment for the wounded; they were the staff. But the front line continually moves backwards. The infantry have played a diminishing role. The last world war was really fought by the so-called staff functions, the back room boys who designed and produced the best weapons. And in a war which is won by the first one to push the button, the key function would be information technology.

As to the second – IT is not the business – it's true computers are not the business, they are general purpose machines. But production tools are not the business, lathes and presses and so on. They can make other products. And the sales force are not the business. They could sell other things. It is a particular production system and a particular sales system that are the business. By the same token it is the company's particular computer systems that are the business. For today's 'just in time' production methods, only the computer can set the stopwatch. Product quality is governed by the use of information technology. Almost every process benefits from computer aided design and manufacturing. Decision making increasingly relies on manipulating computer-based models. More and more, effective selling means capturing suppliers, agents and customers in an information net, on which they come to depend. The very goods themselves are becoming so intimately connected to conditions, instructions and guarantees, that it is becoming hard to tell whether customers buy the product, or the information layer which surrounds it.

As to the third objection, it is easy to say that making and selling are the two primary and distinct things every company has to do. It sounds right – you make something, and then you sell it. The two functions involve different skills, they deal with two distinct sets of people (suppliers and customers), the one follows the other, and both physically touch the goods or services produced. But the supposition rests on what is considered important at the time. In the early days of the industrial revolution, in a world undiscriminatingly hungry for goods, and with newly-discovered machines for making them, production was considered the primary function, and the engineer was king. As capital to fuel the accelerating economy became critical, financial managers climbed onto a throne alongside the engineers. Then goods began to flood the world. Courting the consumer became the game to play, and marketing men moved up onto the board. Then accountants discovered computers. So did production directors. And finally so did the marketing director. In a world where financial models, production and marketing are largely automated, the nature of work, of careers, of the role of human beings in the chain of adding value to things, begins to need reappraisal. Activity divides into two mutually dependant functions: the programmed world of the engine room, and the unstructured, creative world outside. And at last (at last, because there is nowhere further to go), when it becomes the general perception that this is the way things are, two people may well vie for the best seats on the board: the IT director and the human resources director.

So the debate continues. Does responsibility for IT merit a seat on the board? If it does, is it a temporary appointment – a stop gap until the other directors feel comfortable with the subject, and it becomes just another aspect of the traditional making, financing and selling functions? Or is getting IT strategy right so important that it outweighs the other functions and becomes the critical success factor, meriting not only a seat on the board, but perhaps the prime attention of the chief executive himself?

The evidence from those companies using IT as a key component in their strategy is already clear and convincing.

66 We couldn't find any case of a company using computers to gain competitive edge that didn't have an IT champion on the board 99

OVER A HALF OF IT DIRECTORS STATE THAT THEIR POSITION IS TEMPORARY, AND THAT THE RESPONSIBILITY FOR IT WILL EVENTUALLY BE ABSORBED BY THE TRADITIONAL MAIN FUNCTIONS OF THE BUSINESS – PRODUCTION, MARKETING AND FINANCE.

ONE THIRD OF IT DIRECTORS BELIEVE HAVING RESPON-SIBILITY FOR IT MERITS A PERMANENT POSITION ON THE BOARD.

12% OF IT DIRECTORS EXPRESSED THE VIEW THAT IT AND HUMAN RESOURCES WILL REPLACE PRODUCTION AND MARKETING AS THE MAIN ORGANIZATIONAL DIVISIONS IN THE COMPANY AND AT BOARD LEVEL.

Section 2
Where do they come from?

❝An IT director must have an IT background. He must also have strong enough personal qualities to overcome it❞

❝It is the age of the generalist. We can always bring in specialists. But no one ever recruits generalists. They all want specialists❞

❝It can be hampering to have an IT background. Anyone who's specialized in one function can't talk systems as a whole. In the end, you find yourself imposing your will because of your expertise❞

Whether IT should carry board level responsibilities may still be a matter of some debate. But there is one thing over which there is no controversy whatsoever. No one gets there because of his abilities to stand the computer on its head. This is worth dwelling on because the ambitions of many IT executives was to accomplish just this contortion. They were given the job because of their technical skills. It isn't all that surprising that they wished to practice those skills and to improve them.

The unfortunate fact is that there is no promotion in the mainstream hierarchy for any one possessing computer skills alone. The complaint of many IT executives, by-passed in the promotion stakes, is that the computer has become easier to use, and that their skills are no longer valued. There is some truth in this. But the problem for them lies far deeper. No specialist, in the computer field or in any other, can claim a future in management simply on the basis of specialist skills.

The rise of the technician went further in the United States than in any other country. As a consequence, he has had further to fall. A major bank in that country recruited its IT executive from Europe in the early '60s in the van of the 'brain drain' which gathered momentum at that time. The man concerned was not only a first class programmer, he had designed the operating systems and much of the circuitry for one of the pioneering computers produced in the UK, and was among the top 50 computer designers in the world at that time. He was paid a top

❝Once we were magic. We had all the secrets. Now, any kid can program a computer❞

Case

executive salary to start, and given a free hand to automate the bank's administration procedures. A key point is that being in front in the automation race was seen by the bank as a critical success factor, and that people who could put the technology together, and knew enough to be ahead of the game, were in extremely short supply in those days. Following his appointment, technical progress in the bank was both rapid and successful. Before networks were ever offered by the suppliers for example, he had rewired the entire head office skyscraper, not just for computer terminals, but for digital voice as well. By 1987 however, the IT executive was under attack from all sides. In line with the new technology, but also thanks largely to his own successful efforts in distributing computer processing around the company, the users had achieved a measure of independence and were challenging the role of IT at the centre. At the same time the central board were challenging his budget, which was considerably above the industry average because of his strategy of pioneering the technology. He judged the most astute political move he could make was to relinquish the bulk of applications to the users (who were clamouring for this to be done), to appoint his second in command to run the centralized systems that were left, and define a new role for himself. He argued that computers had so elevated the storage, processing and provision of information that they were now one of the main assets of the company, and thus deserving of the specialized attention of a member of the top management team as a key resource in its own right. The bank noted that he was certainly paid as though he were a member of the top management team. So they gave him the title of Chief Information Officer (CIO), and put him on the board. Within two years he was given a handsome settlement and fired. The chief executive commented 'The CIO title is the creation of senior IS managers who are insecure about their job prospects, and who are trying artificially to extend their careers. I hear that nearly a third of top IT men were demoted or fired last year. I can believe it. It's certainly the toughest job in the executive suite right now. There is no way they can survive on their technical knowledge alone. We're a team here. We need business strategies not technology strategies – and people who'll put their salary where their mouths are. Telling us about the technological possibilities for processing information in the next decade, and how we could be left behind, just embarrasses all of us. These guys insist on looking at IT as a profession. While they do that, all they see are its limits. It's time they realized their careers are with the company they work with.'

> **❝** Knowing the technology is not useful. What is useful is knowing the relationship between using it and the business opportunity **❞**

It is probable that most people enter the IT profession because they have an interest in computers, but have no ambition to move into management, let alone to get a seat on the board. There is an archetype

> **❝** I never saw an IT man set the world alight **❞**

technologist who may impress enormously with his knowledge, but who does not inspire the chief executive with his management abilities. It is important, in this connection, to re-examine the statistics of board appointments shown in Figure 3.1 in the previous section. 63% of companies expect to have an IT director by 1993. But this represents the intentions of the chief executive. The same question asked of IT executives produced the figure 48%, only 7% higher than the 1990 level. Which shows that not many more expect to get there. If the chief executives stick to their intentions, where will these directors come from?

The preponderance of those with IT backgrounds is to be expected. What is of interest is that over a third come from a non-IT background. This could well increase. IT people are used to taking technical risk but are not used to situations involving business risk.

They also perceive the dangers of the IT director trap with more apprehension than their colleagues from the more traditional business function. The trap is simple and obvious. The offer of a seat on the board offers involvement with business strategy. But first, he must stop the tail wagging the dog. So he reduces IT to manageable proportions: much is decentralized, some is contracted to outsiders, the rest, greatly demystified, is given to a subordinate.

At this point, he can't go on as a specialist. But if he fails to integrate with the business team, he can't go back. There is nothing to go back to.

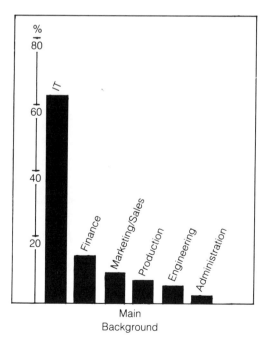

Figure 3.3 Background of IT directors

Three cases illustrate the main routes to the board for IT directors. The clue to choice of background seems to lie in the reasons why each company makes the appointment – what they feel their problem is. The first shows, if not the classic, then certainly the expected case: promotion from within the profession.

Case

Chemical engineers, organized into four divisions with centralized computer service.

Reason for appointment of IT director: Poor service from IT, couldn't recruit skilled IT people, believed a network would improve response to company's requirements, divisions disagreeing on IT strategy, perceived problem was technical – but previous IT manager lacked personality to persuade divisional directors what were the best technical solutions ('IT are not responding to all these problems we're throwing at them').

66 I joined IT as a young man. I thought it would be a fast way to the board! **99**

Background of person appointed: External appointment. Age 48. Trained as mechanical engineer. Programmed computers on engineering applications. Perceived potential of computers and switched career path at 26 to systems analyst with wallpaper manufacturer. Jobs with variety of companies since, as computer project leader, and as data processing manager. Last job: IT executive in a bank, reporting to treasurer at board level.

Mission: Responsible for all policies associated with IT. Responsible for all procurement. To help generate the business plan. To satisfy IT requirements of the business plan.

He said: 'I don't feel I'm a techie. IT has some very technical people these days. It takes seven years to train good systems programmers. I may have been in IT all my life, but now I've only got a gut feel – it's so long since I grappled with the technology at that level.'

The second case shows the appointment of a person from inside the company, and with main strength in the critical performance area of the business. Some previous experience of IT existed, however.

Case

Merchant bank. Single site office.

Reason for appointment of IT director: Banking changed, 60% of funds coming from wholesale market, lending going out on bonds, cross-border trade, all accounts in different currencies, systems not reflecting needs of the bank.

Background of person appointed: Internal appointment. Age 52. Trained as accountant. Two previous positions as administration manager in building society and accountant in another bank. Appointed treasurer in this bank eight years ago. Previous computer manager was asked to leave three years ago. Given responsibility for IT systems at that time, plus administration and the treasury function, and appointed to the board.

> 66 Power comes from a board level appointment plus background knowledge of the business 99

Mission: Total responsibility for all IT. Also, as the principal user of IT systems, responsible for bank performance in certain key areas. To integrate the bank's IT systems with the new trading conditions.

He said: 'I don't think you can be an IT director without some accounting background. This is true, not just in banking, but for manufacturers, travel agents, everyone – we're all counting beans at the end of the day. This may be being ignored today with all this jazz about computers at the front end. Back office computing is the factory, it's about heavy transaction processing, and it's all based on accountancy principles. The front office applications change very fast. But all you can do is bolt these things onto the back shop – you can't change it. The IT man has got to be aware of what's changing in the world, and get the back office set up right. That's what's critical.'

The next case illustrates the appointment of a man whose sole claim to the job was his successful business record.

Case

Food manufacturing group, eight subsidiary companies, some decentralized systems, but mainly centralized computing provided by management services department in group headquarters.

Reason for appointment of IT director: Escalating IT costs and criticism by subsidiary companies concerning value for money, threat to go-it-alone by subsidiaries, profitability declining but strategies confused for lack of control information at centre.

Background of person appointed: Internal appointment. Age 42. Trained in economics and accountancy. Joined group as management trainee in one of their hotels. Various management positions, mainly in inventory, purchasing and distribution. No IT experience. Five years ago appointed managing director of bakeries division.

> 66 The boss was convinced that an IT professional wouldn't have had the nerve to do what I have done 99

Mission: Wrote out own job specification for MD's approval:

Purchasing – 'nothing to move in IT unless I approve it'
Authority – 'report to MD. I want the most powerful committee possible for IT strategy decisions: you, myself, the chairman (the biggest shareholder), the chief accountant (main board member) and one more from the main board.'

Two-year objectives to move existing mainframe to outside facilities management company and run down present systems, install powerful workstations in each company with local systems integrating with a centralized general ledger and sales ledger, and driving a main board executive information system.

He said: 'We had a problem of virtual UDI, strong divisions, each working in isolation. We had to get a handle on the business. Now, all the board papers are automated. They can see the state of fifteen critical success factors, and drill down to the reasons. There's nowhere to hide. And with the new hardware, program maintenance practically eliminated, 20 redundancies; all this has meant a halving of IT costs. No one's complaining about value for money anymore.'

❝ I can't see why a good manager shouldn't manage any function ❞

These three cases, one with an IT background, one from accounting, and one a proven achiever, illustrate that IT directors can come from a variety of previous lives. It seems that the ability to operate at board level is perhaps more important than any particular experience.

'We still haven't created the right animal,' said one IT director. 'The last person you want on the board is someone with a computer science degree. The last person you want is a programmer, up from the ranks. These people won't appreciate why they're there. You can't have the finance man; if he's doing IT well, how's he going to do his finance well? And that's true of all the key functions – matter cannot exist in more than one place at the same time. What do we need? Creativity, vision, the tolerance to accept no, no, no to everything, patient determination, the ability to see the way through problems. This could be any board member. The difference is he must be dedicated to success. Because he is always going to start with failure. His colleagues on the board have not achieved successful use of IT. He is walking into a situation which, on day one, is failure.'

Bringing in an outsider gets over the 'splitting the atom,' problem. But it creates others, particularly in the vital area of trust. One characteristic mentioned more than all the others, and in many cases the fundamental reason for appointing an IT director, was to be able to trust his judgement, in an area where the board felt uncomfortable.

ONLY 18% OF IT DIRECTORS WERE BROUGHT IN FROM
OUTSIDE TO FILL THE APPOINTMENT.

OF THESE, 10% SERVED A PROBATIONARY TERM BEFORE
GETTING A SEAT ON THE BOARD.

Outsiders can also create resentment problems for IT staff. If they're
unable to stand up to these professionals technically, they can be in
trouble.

An Australian bank had its IT department set up, and subsequently
run by a manager with a strong technical background. He retired in
1982, and an outsider was appointed with an audit background. The
bank wanted an outsider's view on spend and the efficiency of the
operation generally. The outsider was replaced after five years by an
internal appointment, a man from the IT department, and with twenty
years operating and systems development experience with the bank.
This man commented 'There was a lot of talk whether to bring in an
outsider. The board was putting on pressure to bring in new blood
at the time. But there are problems with outsiders. It's hard to find
a technician to run a show this size. If you don't get them from an
airline, or one of the other big banks, they won't have experience of
the transaction rates we have here, with over eleven million customers.'
Question: 'They could have appointed an outsider with you as his
adviser?'
'That's exactly what they did in 1982! In fact, there were two of us
advising him. And he'd have been lost without us, I can tell you!
Without IT awareness, he tried to pull the place apart — we don't want
this equipment, it's ridiculous — not realising the availability levels we
need. In fact, it got to the point that the people underneath him had
decided that, if it happened again, they weren't going to be around.
So it was agreed not to make another appointment from outside, and I
was put in.'

There is much in IT that is dictated by fashion. There has been a
plethora of systems development techniques for example, none showing
much gain over another, but installed at great cost and with great
enthusiasm, because they offered new hope in an intractable situation.
Some worried that the trend to appoint IT directors might be just one
such fashion.
It is certainly fashionable today to talk of the hybrid manager as the
ideal candidate, someone with a foot in both camps, a person who has
had both business and IT responsibility. A number of the IT directors
investigated were, in fact, hybrids.

" If he doesn't have
IT skills, he's going to
need one or two very
loyal people to support
him **"**

Case

" IT seemed of
importance in the early
days. Then it went
through a trough. It
became a technical
backwater. In 1985 it
soared back into the
limelight of
importance. Will
another trough
come? **"**

> 10% OF IT DIRECTORS WITH A BUSINESS BACKGROUND
> HAD SOME IT EXPERIENCE AND RESPONSIBILITY BEFORE
> ACCEPTING THE POST.

Few IT directors were discovered who had the reverse experience, that is their main background in IT, but strong business experience as well. Since the main complaint is that we have suffered a surfeit of technology, maybe strength in the business suit is the preferable hand to play.

Since dual experience is the obvious preference, many have jumped on the bandwagon and raised the expected cry 'if it's hybrids we want, let us train them!' Computer courses for businesspeople, and business courses for computerpeople are much in vogue. They are useful. But training doesn't produce the true hybrid. It is job rotation that is needed, and seven years in each function has been stated as the requirement. There are four eras recognizable in the evolution of IT directors:

Dominant Characteristics

Stage I [pre 1980]	An IT man, possibly a genius.
Stage II [circa 1985]	A (brave) business man.
Stage III [present]	A business person, supported by an IT person, as we lean more and more on the technology to enable our business strategies.
Stage IV [2000 onwards]	Hybrids (the real need) begin to populate our boardrooms. A sprinkling of chief executives with IT knowledge becomes noticeable.

> 37% OF IT DIRECTORS STATE THEIR MAIN BACKGROUND IS
> OUTSIDE IT.
>
> 27% OF THOSE RESPONSIBLE FOR TAKING THEIR COMPANY
> INTO THE INFORMATION AGE HAVE NO IT EXPERTISE.
>
> OF ALL IT DIRECTORS SURVEYED, INCLUDING THOSE WITH
> AN IT BACKGROUND, 82% SAID THEY WERE NOT, OR WERE
> NO LONGER, COMPETENT AS COMPUTER SPECIALISTS.
>
> 66% SAID IT EXPERIENCE WAS UNNECESSARY.

Section 3
The problems they face

❝ The problem is the business plan ends up as a series of bullet points. You've nothing you can interpret into an IT strategy ❞

❝ The main problem is you get trapped into timescales. Once you're committed, they say we want three bedrooms, not two. And when you deliver, they say where's the conservatory? ❞

❝ The major problem is we're spending a lot of money, and we know we're going to spend a lot more. But we're getting nothing for it. Nothing you can put dollars on ❞

❝ The real problem is we don't understand the nature of the animal we're trying to manage ❞

It's quite a shopping list. What one would expect in a new function, perhaps. The job isn't well defined, it hasn't been done before, not at board level – and anything viewed from the top looks strange, unfamiliar; new angles appear.

	TECHNICAL	ATTITUDE
EXPRESSED	Time to develop systems	Culture gap
	Getting measured value from IT investments	Users' lack of appreciation of IT
	Insufficiency of corporate objectives	IT professionals' lack of appreciation of the business
SUPPRESSED	Managing novelty and uncertainty	Unacceptance at board level

Figure 3.4   Classification of IT directors' problems

Two ways of categorizing the IT director's problems suggest themselves for the purpose of analysis. There are problems of technique: problems, that is, with the way we do things, ways which aren't producing the wanted answers for IT managers. And there are attitude problems, problems connected with the way IT professionals, the users, top management and the punters perceive or ignore the information revolution. Another, and in many ways more interesting, classification is into the expressed, openly discussed and talked-about problems, and those seldom voiced, and which, when discussed, seem to emerge over drinks rather than on conference platforms.

The matrix in Figure 3.4 shows that the IT directors' main problems assort themselves evenly into the groupings suggested. Taking the expressed problems first, a recent survey showed that the directors concerned rated them in the order of importance shown in Figure 3.5.

The three main technical problems are no surprise to anyone who has worked in IT in business. What may come as a surprise is that the technical problems are not all at the top of the list.

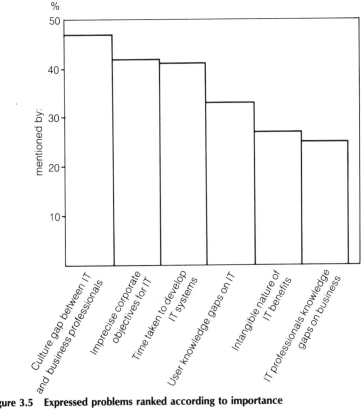

Figure 3.5 Expressed problems ranked according to importance

Bridging the so-called culture gap between the IT users, and the IT knowledge workers, who implement the computer systems and often impose them onto the users, is held to be the major difficulty.

Taking the technical problems first, the one apparently presenting the major difficulty is the entirely different level of detail presented by the corporate plan, and required of an IT plan.

IT directors brought up in an IT environment are nurtured on the need for precise plans, for requirements to be stated in full, with no 'i's left to be dotted, no 't's left to be crossed, and, above all, to make up your mind and stick to it – no last minute revisions, no change of heart. Even those without an IT background, faced with the requirement of a rule following machine to have all the rules spelled out, soon perceive this need.

But their colleagues on the board produce more sketchy plans. They are doing no more than is natural to human beings. Such sketchy, or bullet point, plans are very suitable for human control systems – where a statement of objectives, rather than the detailed steps to take, are not only sufficient but better, since they leave people free to use their skills to think on their feet. It is often called 'seat of the pants' management, and decried by IT management. Rightly, since they cannot manage inflexible computer systems in that way.

But we should not forget that, whilst it has unacceptable shortcomings for IT planning, it has tremendous virtues for people, especially in a world driven by progress and determined to change the rules of the game at shorter and shorter intervals.

> **“** They can't plan – a plan for them is go or no go **”**

'No plan withstands contact with the enemy'. These words were said by a German general at the time of the First World War. Today, he would be dismayed by the number of plans that never even make contact. The shortening of the business planning horizon on the one hand, to enable the business to think on its feet; and the lengthening of the period needed to implement IT plans on the other, with the complex systems integrations and communications involved as the technology advances; both throw the two planning mechanisms further and further out of kilter.

The second technical problem is closely connected with the one just described. This second problem, that of the time and cost of developing and delivering computer programs, is aggravated by the situation of unclear and changing requirements. Managers complain they are shooting at a moving target.

> **“** If I were honest when we start a system, we'd never start **”**

It is also the case that much of the work in developing a computer system is pioneering. The technology is changing so fast that a part of it is always unfamiliar to the development staff. It is also, by definition, the first time that the system being put onto the computer has been automated. No one really knows what the effects will be. 'It is an engineered product of quite fundamental complexity, it takes a very long time to build, and it is also ridiculous to assume we should have the luck to get it right first time!'

The research nature of the work is commonly overlooked by management, sometimes willingly, sometimes it is deliberately concealed.

There is no escaping the fact that under present methods of systems development, the job takes a very long time. And, to make it worse, it demands high skills and experience levels, which are in short supply.

To overcome the problem, packaged software, which can be bought off the shelf, has been tried. It triggered off a new phase in the information revolution, since the users, unable to write their own programs, could none the less by-pass the centralized IT department and do their own thing by buying packages.

They have had little impact on the large centralized systems however, particularly and obviously so in areas where a company is trying to compete and distinguish itself from others, since packages offer a standard solution.

There is a present swing to using outside contractors, because of the skills shortage, and the problem of retaining skilled staff in house. Controlling a largely outsourced function gives rise to fresh management problems however.

And so it goes, on and on, an endless mention of difficulties. For a problem to have remained intractable for so long, impervious apparently to management's efforts to solve it, must say something about its nature.

MEETING PROJECT DEADLINES WAS THE UNCHALLENGED TOP WORRY FOR IT MANAGEMENT FOR TEN YEARS UNTIL 1989. SINCE THEN IT HAS NOT GONE AWAY. IT HAS BEEN RELEGATED TO SECOND PLACE BY THE PROBLEM OF WHAT PROJECTS SHOULD BE ATTEMPTED.

The third technical problem is stated to be the intangible nature of computer benefits.

The difficulty is clear. In order to justify our investment in IT we need to write something down on the right-hand side of the cost/benefit analysis. The value of what we are about to receive should exceed what we are about to spend, or we shouldn't spend it. If a dose of IT is about saving some costs we are already incurring, that is doing exactly what we are doing now, but cheaper, then we can write something down in the benefits column. We can write down the savings. But if it is about enabling us to do something new, we can't. Because it is new, we don't know what will happen.

Stated as the difficulty of intangible benefits, the problem seems to be a technical one. It has inspired many to study new ways of measuring benefits.

Nothing satisfactory has yet emerged, however. And there are some who are beginning to say that the problem is not the technical one of measurement. It may be an attitude problem: that of value for money. Are we always able to write down what value we put on things? As Grahame Greene reminds us, 'There is no such thing as value. There is only the price people are prepared to pay.'

66 Anyone who doesn't see that value for money is the main problem in IT isn't using it sufficiently to experience the point. They're still in the stage of replacing people with technology. It's when you start supporting people with technology that the problem starts 99

66 I won't accept you can't put a price on it 99

These three technical problems, and they are amongst the top six difficulties facing IT directors, have one thing in common. They are each examples of where established management techniques, employed successfully in the era of the industrial revolution, are failing when applied in the information revolution.

What characterized the industrial revolution was the total reliance on human beings to manage it. When the human brain was the only instrument of control, success attended those with the courage, determination and judgement to attack and solve problems as they arose from day to day, and who were quick on their feet when they found out they were wrong. Planning techniques consisted of setting goals and then playing much of it by ear. Performing was largely about applying the right level of resources and of motivating people. And investing was about backing your judgement.

Today, these techniques have been refined, but they have not changed fundamentally. What has changed, however, is the way we control organizations. This function we now share with machines. And the management techniques developed for a past era are now being found wanting by IT directors. Our plans aren't precise enough. We can't build systems quickly enough, and our cost/benefit analyses aren't robust enough.

If, as has been suggested, business is about to be divided into two primary areas, that handled by people and that handled by machines, then the part handled by machines clearly needs some new management techniques to be developed.

As to the attitude problems, however difficult they may be to bridge, the knowledge gaps of both users and technicians about each other's territory is relatively straightforward to describe. IT is new, hardly a generation old, and those who have not made it their profession not only do not appreciate its capability, they are, to a great extent, understandably afraid of it. Most IT directors regret those attempts made to overcome this, which consist of humanizing the machine. 'Whilst we attribute human characteristics to the computer, memory, intelligence and so on, we will fail to treat it as a highly engineered product.'

66 It speaks COBOL doesn't it? **99**

The knowledge gap of the technicians is frequently misrepresented, however. It is not so much that they do not know what is going on in the business. Indeed, since their job is to investigate the business systems, they are sometimes the most knowledgeable in this area. It is more that they do not know why these systems are going on, that they work from an analysis of what is, rather than what should be, that they seek to automate from the point of view of processing efficiency rather than business effectiveness.

66 I think it is a load of rubbish that IT people don't understand the business. My analysts know more about the accounts and billing system than the accountants. They've analyzed it from the bottom up. And they move around, finance one week, marketing the next. They see the overall picture ❯❯

❮❮ They think their department is the most important in the firm. Technical jealousies dominate their thinking – they all have different views. But how to get a better business achievement wouldn't enter their heads ❯❯

In short, they are not part of the business – and many do not want to be. Motivation gap rather than knowledge gap might be a better term.

> THE TOP PROBLEM FOR IT DIRECTORS IN ALL COUNTRIES SURVEYED WAS NOT A TECHNICAL DIFFICULTY, IT WAS THE CULTURE GAP BETWEEN THOSE WHO BELIEVED THEY WERE FACING AN INFORMATION REVOLUTION AND THOSE ACCUSED OF LOOKING THE OTHER WAY.

The main attitude problem, which outweighs all the technical problems as well, according to the survey, was expressed as the culture gap.

In view of its importance, the next chapter focuses on this topic in detail. For the moment however, a brief analysis of what this problem really is might be helpful, since the term used to describe it is somewhat confusing.

It is not a problem of understanding, either of the technology or of its products: knowledge, communication and automation. It is the gap between those who judge these products on how they improve the existing business, and those who believe they will change the way business is done.

One IT director expressed it as follows: 'There is no benefit in computerizing the jobs we do at present,' he said. 'Fortunately, we cannot do it. When we try, it is doubtful whether we save enough people to justify the investment. But what is certain, once we have computerized a job we used to do by hand, we no longer do it in the same way. Production and selling become standardized. The job of humans then becomes supplying the personal touches which make the standards work.'

❮❮ He said 'That's not an IT issue, it's an organizational issue'. It was a clear hands-off sign ❯❯

This is a quite fundamental change. If true, it changes the nature of competition, the extent the value chain can be integrated, the whole purpose of work. And the possibility that it is true polarizes management into two cultures: those who believe it, and try to act accordingly, and those who, whatever their belief, act as though each fresh dose of IT should do no more than jack up the efficiency of the present operations.

The problem, for the IT director, is that his computer systems permeate all the activities of the organization, that whatever he does therefore, affects the roles and responsibilities of his colleagues on the board, and this is a job he cannot do whilst there is a major gap in the perception of what his job is.

❮❮ Will we all look back in years to come and say, well, it was

So much for the problems revealed by formal surveys. They seem profound enough to merit the epithet 'the toughest job in the executive suite right now' conferred by the chief executive in the last chapter.

Face to face discussions with a number of IT directors revealed two further problems however, which have not so far received much publicity.

The first reveals concerns over the vulnerability of organizations today, as they come to depend more and more on computer systems which, it was suggested, may be inherently unmanageable.

A large financial institution in the United States had begun to install computer systems in 1958. It was possible to recognize three stages in the evolution of these systems. Stage one was the development of a succession of systems automating the basic operation in the bank, which was maintaining the customers' accounts. These successive systems involved two complete rewrites in the early days, since the hardware used changed fundamentally and the systems designed for one machine would not work on its replacement. By 1969 however, the system had become too large and complex for it to be either an economical or practical proposition to rewrite again. Since then, the strategy had been to make appropriate changes to the existing system to preserve its life. These changes consisted of add-ons to satisfy new user requirements, and alterations to make it run on more modern, larger and more powerful computers.

The second stage was to connect this system to remote terminals so that the users could operate much of the system themselves. The third stage was to develop a number of satellite systems and then to interconnect the basic customer accounting system with these satellites and with other systems operated by outside organizations.

Interviewed in 1990, the IT director stated his major concern was how the fabric of the organization would hold together in the future, now that it depended on the 'quicksand of computer software'. 'There is a great danger,' he said, 'in thinking that the culture gap problem will be solved in the ways suggested by the popular press. More computer graduates, more home computers and soon we shall all be computer-literate. But the gap between university computing and the workings of IT in a sizeable organization like this is a mile wide. It's the nature of large software infrastructures, which we build and then no longer understand, that has to be appreciated. Let me give you four worries I have to live with.

1) *Our limitations and frailty*

We inherit our backbone systems today. Our predecessors designed and built them. They have grown to a no-longer-comprehensible degree of complexity. When they work, they run the show. When they don't, there is really nothing we can do about it anymore. Not quickly anyway. We just have to hope that time will always be on our side.

an interesting idea. Taking all the social and business infrastructures in the world, and automating them. It didn't work; but it was an interesting idea **99**

Case

2) *Fraud and penetration*

It is frankly not too difficult to break in to computer systems. The people who build systems will always be able to penetrate them. They're the same skills. Getting at manual systems requires collusion, because they're spread around. But these giant brain boxes are all interconnected, and operate automatically, untouched by human hand. There are some very big frauds being investigated right now. We just spent over half a billion dollars investigating a virus in our mainframe.

3) *Engineering change*

The domino effect of knocking down one card, when each system impinges on 25 others, of tampering with something no longer understandable, makes engineering changes and further development a new science. Throwing more and more resources at the problem makes it worse. Each extra person involved increases the complexity. But investing more resources is a natural management reaction. In our frustration it is almost all we can do. The trouble is that, unless we all agree to call a halt to progress, major changes in our systems are needed for survival in the market place.

4) *Testing*

As IT director, I an responsible for something which can no longer be tested – the paths through the software are too numerous to investigate the effect of each change we make. So we go live with only a fifty per cent level of confidence. We don't yet have the management techniques or attitudes to live with this sort of situation.'

The second, seldom-voiced but clearly often experienced problem to emerge during interviews concerned the acceptance of the position of IT director. 'My main problem,' said one, 'in doing my job the way I think I should do my job is the subtle resistance of more powerful directors. You've got to be strong willed enough to hang on in there. The easy thing would be to do the efficiency job they all seem to want me to do. You asked me about a book on managing IT at Board level, resulting from this research – and what would disappoint me about it. I'd be most disappointed if it said the day of the IT director has come. That is not the case. There are too many difficulties in the way at the moment.'

> 26% OF IT DIRECTORS EXPRESSED THEIR CONCERN THAT THE BASIC SYSTEMS INFRA-STRUCTURES ON WHICH COMPANIES NOW DEPEND WERE BECOMING UNMANAGEABLE.
>
> 56% FELT THAT THEIR POSITION AND ROLE WERE NOT ACCEPTED BY THE MAJORITY OF THE BOARD.

Section 4
The hidden agenda

❝My overt role is to support a strategic direction. This direction is business led. But the business lead only makes sense if the business is aware of what IT can do. So my real role is to create that awareness❞

❝I was appointed to hold down the costs. What I've done is to build a new IT infrastructure that will give us survival chances as the information revolution takes off. Fortunately the new computers we're using cost less than the old ones. That's the only reason I got approval❞

❝Short-termism governs our share prices. It governs our decisions, and our investment policies. The trick in IT is to build the long-term survival structure using profitable short-term bricks. This way, you don't need to bridge the culture gap, because you've got instant agreement❞

This section is about the job IT directors do. But it is really about two jobs, or two different perceptions of their job: what they do, and what their board colleagues think they do.

> WITH ONE EXCEPTION, EVERY IT DIRECTOR INTERVIEWED HAD A HIDDEN AGENDA. EACH WAS ARRIVED AT INDEPENDENTLY. BUT EVERY ONE WAS THE SAME.

This statement is designed to appease the reader who believes he also is that exception. But it is a lie. The truth is, every IT director we interviewed had a secret agenda. Before discussing detailed roles however, both spoken and unspoken, some notes on organization – where IT directors fit, and how they operate – are appropriate.

Clearly, no company has the same organization structure. The main differences found with respect to the positioning and roles of IT directors were, firstly, whether they combined the role with responsibility for another function (and, if so, which one), and secondly, differences between small and medium-sized companies on the one hand, and large companies, groups and multinationals on the other.

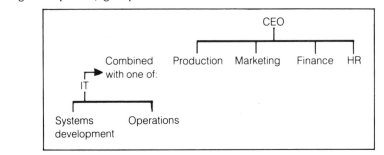

Figure 3.6   Organization structures: small to medium companies

The smaller companies typically exhibit less decentralization of IT than large ones; and the role of the IT director tends to be more all-embracing therefore, covering not only IT strategy and planning, but also the provision of most of the data processing service, with responsibility for efficiency, levels of service and so on. Due to the small size of the board, if IT is represented at the top level in such companies, it automatically gets intimately involved with corporate objectives and strategy planning.

For the same reason however, the function is often combined with one of the more traditional board level responsibilities. Finance and production were the most common job-sharing candidates.

In the case of finance, the reasons seemed to lie in the origins of computer applications. IT grew up in administration and the finance director was its natural early protagonist.

The reason for combining it with production (of goods or services) or marketing lay in answering the question: where was the main strategic use of IT being made by the company concerned? IT was combined with marketing in only 10% of companies studied.

The IT function itself was typically split into systems development and the day-to-day provision of computer services. Where a substantial amount of data processing was carried out by the users however, a user advisory group was occasionally found.

22% OF THE IT BUDGET WAS SPENT BY THE USERS IN COMPANIES EMPLOYING UNDER 10,000.

IN LARGER COMPANIES THIS DECENTRALIZED SPEND ROSE TO 37%.

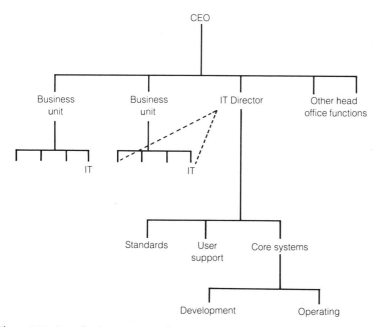

Figure 3.7   Organization structures: large companies

In larger companies, the role exhibits far greater variety, and so does the positioning of the IT director in the organization structure. The primary factor governing this variety is the degree of decentralization that has taken place.

Also of great influence however is the extent to which an organization is intent on pursuing vertical or horizontal integration. The prime enabler of these extensions of the value chain is IT, particularly the use of electronic data interchange where the links in the value chain become electronic rather than relying on the transmission of paper.

A further strong influence on organizational structure is the perception of growth in terms of turnover and in extending the value chain control span, but at the same time reducing rather than increasing the number of those directly employed. Again, automation is the prime enabler, but hand in glove co-operation between IT and human resources becomes of the essence.

The chart reproduced in Figure 3.8 is not so much an archetype of the large company organization structures found. It is more an embodiment of the key ideas regarding IT directorships that are currently being tried out, and thus serves to illustrate the purpose of these organizational experiments.

The distinction between line and support roles is maintained. The line responsibilities are for complete supply chains however, involving several subsidiary or more loosely related companies. Each of these companies (in practice they might be divisions, not fully fledged companies) has its

66 Human resources and IT are the lead functions today. They are leading the information revolution, which redefines growth, not as a process which moves from the employment of a hundred to the employment of two hundred, but as a process enabling a hundred, struggling with a business bottleneck, to function more effectively as twenty **99**

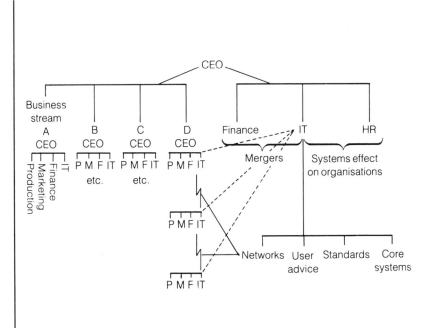

Figure 3.8 Organization structure in company pursuing vertical and horizontal integration through IT

own IT executive who reports to the chief executive of that company. They have a functional responsibility to the group IT director however, for standards and interfaces and approval of major applications.

The group IT director has a twin role with the group finance director regarding acquisitions, mergers and special relationships, with specific responsibility for investigating and recommending systems integrations.

He has a twin role with the human resources director regarding all systems changes, and their effects on employment and organization structure.

He has the specific responsibility for all intercompany and interdivision networks. He is responsible for specifying group IT standards, and advising users on developing and running their own applications. He is responsible for designing, laying down and running the group's core systems, which are shared or fed by member companies.

> 74% OF IT DIRECTORS USE FORMAL COMPUTER STEERING COMMITTEES TO DETERMINE STRATEGY.

Committee structures are commonly used in organizations. They are usually formed to plan and monitor activities which involve many departments, or activities which are not the specific responsibility of any department. In other words, they deal with things that fall outside the normal management hierarchy.

It appears to be a characteristic of computer management, however, that many of the key roles, part of day-to-day management in other departments, are undertaken through committees.

A European manufacturing company identified five key functions in IT which demanded action in other departments, and sometimes across the company, if they were to be successful. They were:

1) *Project management*
   All systems development work undertaken in the computer department takes place on behalf of the users. All systems involve reorganization of the user departments to some degree. The users drive the systems to the extent that they enter data and demand outputs. The users own, or share ownership of, the records to be held in the computer database. It is the users' requirements that are to be automated. It is the users who will bear the costs and must reap the benefits.

2) *Big stick*
   Some systems are for the benefit of the company rather than the particular user who is required to put in effort to develop and run it, perhaps to reorganize and even to give up some control because of it, maybe even to pay for it. In such cases, the insistence of the chief executive may be needed, to develop and implement the system.

3) *Priorities*
   User initiatives for systems development and maintenance improvements place demands on the limited systems development resources in the computer department. Rationing and priority schemes need to be implemented. These affect all users of computer services.

4) *Service levels*
   Once service level agreements have been reached with the users, there is a need to monitor achievements. This monitoring should be a joint process amongst all users, since computer operating priorities, capacity scheduling and operating difficulties affect them all.

5) *Policy and objectives*
   Policies, particularly concerning standards, and IT objectives affect all areas of the company.

66 The first thing I did was to form the most powerful committee, the four people without whom nothing moves **99**

Case

66 The top executive committee is the breakthrough! **99**

These needs for common action caused the IT director to institute a three-tier system of committees. A chief executive's committee, including most of the board, met at three-monthly intervals, to agree policy and objectives, to discuss conflicts of interest and to rule on disagreements and action required. The IT director chaired two other committees which met each month. One consisted of all the project managers, and reported progress, identified problems and agreed action. The other consisted of the heads of all user departments, and reported achievements against service level agreements and set priorities for proposed systems developments.

This case ostensibly illustrates the needs for co-ordinated action, often more in the interests of the company as a whole than of any individual user, which permeate the management problems of the IT director.

It is important however to observe that committees are also proliferated for another, underlying reason. Educate is such an offputting word. The implications that the educator is in a somewhat superior state, and that the recipients are uneducated, are hard to avoid.

Nevertheless, the culture gap problem, discussed in the last section, is the biggest barrier to the successful use of IT – and committees which cross the cultural boundary, and expose the nature and workings of the IT animal, continually illustrating them by current examples drawn from the committee members' own departments, are seized by many IT directors as vehicles to inform their colleagues of the management problems, the shortcomings, and the opportunities presented by IT.

The need to manage a function by committee, however, raises interesting questions about the longer-term viability of the function as a separate identity. Committees can provide excellent vehicles for abrogating responsibility. In the last analysis, it has been argued, the role of the IT director is no more than to provide a chairman for the endless committees formed to resolve the difficulties of systems which are for the benefit of all, but for no one in particular.

Third on the list of the main jobs that IT directors are appointed to do (see Figure 3.9) is ensuring the efficient provision of IT services.

Two things make the task worthy of comment. Firstly it involves running highly technical and complicated equipment. Nothing strange about that; don't most production processes involve managing technical, complicated machinery? What distinguishes computer processing in this respect is that the technical processes involved are not related to the nature of the product or services provided by the company. They are not understood, not part of the corporate culture in the way that a lathe is part of a joinery works, an oven is part of a bakery. They are also not directly related to the company's output. So, short of breakdown, there is no immediate and readily understandable way for the board to know whether things in the computer room are being run efficiently or not.

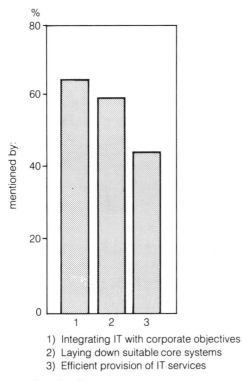

1) Integrating IT with corporate objectives
2) Laying down suitable core systems
3) Efficient provision of IT services

Figure 3.9   Main roles of IT directors

The appointment of a director rather than a technician to be responsible for this function comes back once again to the question of trust. If we can't judge performance, then let's appoint someone whose judgement we can accept to devote his time to the problem.

The basic techniques employed to achieve and maintain efficiency are to do no more than apply management techniques already proven in other areas of the business – that is, to establish units of output (invoices produced, database accesses etc.) and to ascertain and control the costs of each of these units produced.

These measures are increasingly set as prices in service agreements signed with the users. Once a service department is set up to charge for its services under freely negotiated contracts however, it gets to look more and more like a separate business. Users are free in many cases to seek competitive prices outside the organization.

The issue has to be faced, of whether a department we don't understand, which employs skills foreign to the business, and whose

66 Arms-length price negotiation is a fiction. If the users are free to go elsewhere, then the computer department must be free to sell outside to recover the lost business. And who's picking up the bill for the common infrastructure and investments in new technology? It's no good pretending it's

a separate business – it should actually be one **99**

66 The prime function of this business is no longer making and selling the product, it is installing and running the information technology that does these things for us. To let another company run this function for us is to abdicate our most important responsibility **99**

66 What is important about core system thinking: it provides a rationale for what should be centralized and what decentralized instead of leaving it to power politics, it automatically ensures all applications are integrated, and

outputs are so remote from what the company is there to do, should really be a part of the company. The difficulty with price fixing is that so much of the costs are common to all applications. It is also hard to build in margins to cover keeping the company's equipment up to date, and yet hold prices competitive at the same time. A number of IT directors are contracting out this role, employing facilities management companies to run their computers for them.

The second main role, and rated considerably more important than the efficiency question just discussed, is designing and laying down core systems. The concept of the core system is the most important development in IT management's thinking to have emerged so far, and merits a chapter to itself later on (The future of the centralized IT department).

For the first thirty years of the information revolution, computer applications were seen as distinct entities. Developing complete systems for each of these applications was seen as the main job of the computer department. Towards the end of the '60s, it became clear that all these applications were really interrelated; they shared information and processing facilities.

The first reaction to this discovery was to build bigger and bigger systems – ideally: one enormous system that would embrace all the applications of the company. These attempts, although, with hindsight, clearly impractical, continued for many years, and have provided a legacy of monster systems too inflexible to change and which saddle most of today's large organizations.

Programs, once written, are exceedingly difficult to change. Large programs greatly exacerbate this difficulty. They also take for ever to develop. And no one can visualize their requirements on so vast a scale – so the larger the program, the worse the system specification. But worst of all, the interrelationships in large systems increase logarithmically, so that a point is soon reached where the system can neither be satisfactorily tested nor understood.

Soon after Watershed, a new idea for systems development emerged. The idea splits the development of computer systems into two distinct parts.

First a core system is laid down. This consists of the updating of the company's common databases, running the one or two high volume transaction processing jobs which feed this database, and providing the company's communications infrastructure.

Applications, often developed by the users themselves, are subsequently hung onto this core.

Laying down these cores is very properly a board level concern. It consumes over three-quarters of the IT budget, it is the one area of IT which is genuinely supra-department, since all depend on it but none can justify it on their own, and it is the fundamental part of the company's IT system where success or failure will affect corporate survival.

The top job for the IT director however is claimed to be integrating IT with corporate objectives. It is easy to say. It is obviously to be done. Why hasn't it been done? What is it about this trite and obvious precept that makes it the prime reason for the appointment of IT directors? The following case illustrates some of the problems to be solved in order to achieve this integration.

once the core is in place, users can think of application developments taking place in time to meet their current plans instead of the two and three year marathons we used to suffer **99**

Case

A US food manufacturer installed their first computer in the early 1960s. Throughout the 60s and 70s, its prime application was to streamline the administration systems of the company. Challenged in 1985 to show a measured contribution to the company's business objectives, the IT executive was frankly astonished. 'There is no direct correspondence between the company's objectives and the computer objectives,' he said. 'We are here to automate the administration procedures. We save clerks, we save money, we speed up data processing, we make information available. These things are so obviously needed they don't merit the status of corporate objectives. We just get on with it. It's a continual job.' Pressed further to analyze his role in achieving the company's clearly stated objectives, he stated that there was nothing specific the computer did in this connection, since the users did not appreciate its potential sufficiently to raise their sights and target onto the new possibilities it offered – and anyway they always set objectives for the current year, and computer systems just couldn't be revamped in that sort of timescale.

These three things – computers confined to the back office, failure to appreciate IT's potential and the failure to develop systems within the business planning timescale – are now being challenged by the board. Since 1985, there has been continual talk of the use of computers for gaining competitive edge. The exposure of such benefits as shortlived has not deterred a steady shift towards the application of the computer in the front shop of the company, often just to keep up with new ways of producing, selling and doing business.

OVER ONE THIRD OF ALL COMPUTER APPLICATIONS ARE NOW IN THE AREAS OF PRODUCTION AND MARKETING.

Provided suitable core systems are in place, user applications can be developed rapidly to fit in with today's need to be flexible in the market place.

The key difficulty remaining is the lack of perception, at top management level, of the potential of information technology to improve business performance, and thus to be a prime mover rather than a support in setting objectives in the first place. Providing this perception is the main role of the IT director, and perhaps the main reason why he needs to be a director, helping to navigate rather than just improving things in the engine room.

When we look at the low scoring jobs however, represented in Figure 3.10, it is clear that those questioning the viability of the IT director's position have ammunition in plenty to fire.

Only 11% claimed that they had the responsibility for initiating IT systems. And this despite the universal acknowledgement of the culture gap, and the complaint that the users had insufficient perception of the potential of IT to initiate anything for themselves. What claim to a seat on the board can be sustained by those paid not to have ideas?

What claim to be a director can be sustained by those not responsible for the payoff from the investments they control? Those with specific responsibility for payoff are very few and far between — mainly those combining responsibility for IT with that for a line function. The marketing director for example, who said 'I'm an IT supremo, who also has the responsibility for running that part of the business which is dominated by the systems I've installed'.

The most disturbing thing in the 'not my patch' list however is the astonishingly low number who claim to have a specific responsibility for predicting the effect of IT on business methods.

We have discussed the importance of a company's core system — its IT infrastructure on which its future business capability depends. These systems represent major investments. More important they can take as much as five years to lay down. Most important, they are extremely difficult to change. The excellence or deficiencies of the core system is what competitive advantage will all be about in ten years' time. How can an IT director satisfactorily accept responsibility for building the core system without a knowledge of the business conditions he is building it for?

These objections are successfully parried, since these two vital functions, initiating strategies and predicting the effect of IT, although not ostensibly in the IT director's job description, are nevertheless all being performed.

It seems that today's IT directors have to maintain what is virtually

❝ The only business case I can make on my own is to improve IT efficiency **❞**

❝ The reason you want to do something with IT is a business reason. So it's appropriate that a business executive is responsible for the payoff **❞**

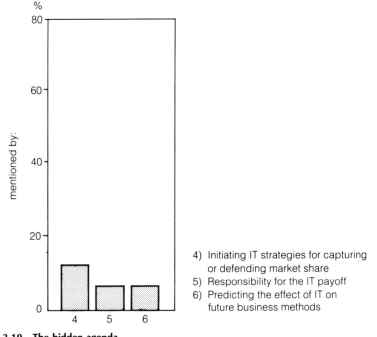

4) Initiating IT strategies for capturing
   or defending market share
5) Responsibility for the IT payoff
6) Predicting the effect of IT on
   future business methods

Figure 3.10   The hidden agenda

a hidden agenda. And it has to do with the culture gap. Not only do their colleagues have difficulty accepting that they should be influential members of the board, (compared with, say, production, marketing and finance), they are denied the power to become one since they are not given responsibility, off their own bats, for the two things that guarantee power: spending money and bringing it in.

The true role in the long term for the IT director, as perceived by those doing the job at present, is to have responsibility for the strategic use of IT. This means responsibility for IT infrastructures and policies which further corporate strategies. It means sharing the responsibility for formulating those strategies. It means sharing the responsibility for business performance in pursuing those strategies.

It also means sharing the power needed to carry out these responsibilities. This seems to be what is lacking. In its absence, a spectrum of approaches was discovered which enables IT directors to pursue what they believe to be their true role, as a hidden agenda.

At one end of the spectrum, there is what might be called the *laissez-faire* approach.

A large US engineering firm had appointed an IT director with the objectives of containing escalating costs. The director identified

Case

several cost reduction strategies, and had achieved savings which had clearly satisfied the board. He perceived opportunities for business improvements by increasing the IT spend however. In the belief that only line management could actually make use of these opportunities, and thus approve the IT systems involved, he ran a series of senior management education programs. At first, IT was an unknown quantity, and they were keen to learn. But after the initial course, they no longer saw it as a problem, just an enabling technology like photocopying. They failed, in the IT director's eyes, to see that it raised management problems that they must own. He then gave a presentation, demonstrating that a substantial section of the company's business would be threatened if they did not conform to the Computer Aided Logistics System likely to become mandatory for US Department of Defense contracts. This resulted in a strategy debate that lasted several months, but in the end did not result in installing the necessary computer systems. The IT director commented on his role, saying 'I've cut the costs. The users are happy. As far as the board are concerned I've done my job. I could get time on the agenda, but what's the point? It would only irritate them. So I work to change attitudes, whittling away at the culture gap by describing IT opportunities and threats.'

❝ I seek to change attitudes ❞

To an investigator, this seems a doubtful approach. It is important to record however, that it is the majority situation. Most IT directors, no matter how convinced of the significance of the information revolution, and of the fundamental impact it must have on their company, seek to influence corporate policy by discussion, formal presentations and the preparation of papers for circulation amongst top management.

During our investigation, we saw hundreds of such papers, stacked importantly along the shelves in the IT director's office, but filed, unread, by his senior colleagues.

Five more approaches were identified each illustrating the use of successively stronger and more positive action by the IT director.

Case

❝ There are three stages in the evolution of IT. I'm preparing for stage three ❞

Prepare the ground: One company had decentralized its IT almost entirely. The IT director stated this was his policy since it was necessary for the users to experience both the potential and the shortcomings of IT for themselves in order to bridge the culture gap. 'There are three successive stages in the development of IT,' he said. ' The first recognizes that IT is separate and across the board, and centralizes it. The second recognizes that if decentralized business units are to perform, and be held responsible for their performance, they must be responsible for their own computers. The third stage takes place when the users realize that they can't cope with some things, that some systems must be provided at corporate level and that standards are needed to integrate the company's separate information systems. My role is to specify standards, formulate policies, and design interfaces and core systems in preparation for that day.'

Hybrid systems: A public utility appointed an IT director to examine the IT spend, reduce it where possible and satisfy the board they were getting value for money on the remainder. The company worked on the principle of only investing in IT if tangible benefits could be identified. They sought major staff reductions and looked to IT to achieve them. The director quickly came to the conclusion that the most important part of the IT spend could not be justified in that way. The staff savings precept restricted applications to the automation of the existing organization and methods. He also perceived that his colleagues would be uncomfortable with investment proposals based on strategic benefits since they cut across departmental boundaries, and the benefits frequently arose outside the department making the investment. Furthermore the benefits could not be measured – they involved business risk, and in the unknown areas of systems, rather than in the familiar areas of production and marketing. He adopted the approach of implementing hybrid systems therefore: systems which were half-hard in terms of benefits. He gave the example of the delivery system which handled billings on terminals in the sales office, and was justified on the basis of consequent clerical savings in the billings department. In addition to automating the billings process however, the system used a scratchpad to produce negotiating briefs and client contracts. 'We began to use the new billings system to enhance the sales system,' he said. 'Paying accounts became a sales opportunity. This was competitive edge stuff. The point is this wasn't the specified objective of the system. We rode in the real benefits on the back of the objective to save some clerks.'

Responsible for integration: 'My perceived role was to improve the responsiveness of IT to business problems. This leads to short-termism. You're curing symptoms, building small, individual, stop-gap systems, instead of getting to the heart of the disease by building strategic systems which go across the board. Everything encourages short-termism in IT – the business planning cycle which demands systems within the year, sometimes within a month, and the constant fight against take over – long term investment does nothing for the share prices. I can't change these attitudes. There is acceptance that the same information is used by several departments however. Based on this, I have succeeded in getting my role enlarged to include responsibility for integration. Whenever I'm asked to put in a system because someone's

Case

66 I ride in the systems we need on the back of the systems they want 99

Case

66 My life's a constant attack on short-termism 99

feeling a pain, I now take the opportunity to build a common solution. Later, when someone else catches the pain, I've got the cure ready. Little by little, we're building an across the board infrastructure.'

Case

❝ I painted the future. He wanted it now **❞**

Superstructure before infrastructure: In a company where the IT director was appointed to make the computer systems responsive to business needs, the typical symptoms of board level abdication from the problem existed, namely: uncontrolled cost escalation, unacceptable time scales for systems development, and a bottom-up approach to defining requirements lead by initiatives from the IT department rather than the users. The director's plan was to farm out the existing systems, with their heavy maintenance problems, to a facilities management company, meanwhile rebuilding them from scratch using a centralized core system with powerful user workstations, phasing out the old system in stages as the rebuilding took place. The project was planned to take four years. He was unable to persuade his colleagues to go ahead with the scheme. 'You've got to shortcut building the core system. We need the information now,' said the chief executive. The IT director therefore installed an Executive Information System in the board room, and took the existing board papers (an eighty page monthly report which contained manually compiled performance reports for all divisions) and fed them into the computer. No board papers were issued any more. The directors probed the group's performance by interrogating the computer at whatever level of detail they needed to know. The system was an immediate success, and the IT director was voted substantial funds to automate the manual preparation of the performance reports over a four year period. 'Give people what they want,' he said, 'and they're on your side. What they don't realize is that the automation improvements they've now authorized give us the chance to build the IT infrastructure that they still don't see the need for!'

Case

❝ Phase I is doing what we do better. Phase II, doing things in new ways, is on the hidden agenda **❞**

Centralize IT, decentralize IS: One IT director was appointed to reorganize IT so that it contributed to the company's objectives. Working with his colleagues, he identified objectives in the six key areas of:

  return on capital
  risk management
  marketing
  selling
  infrastructures
  customer service levels

Critical Success Factors were set in each area. The information required to monitor these factors was identified. The data sources from which the construction of this information was possible were defined, and the systems put in place to support a database in each of the key areas. Whilst this work had the support of his top management colleagues, the IT director stated that in his view it was only stage one, and that he was really working to enable an undiscussed stage two to take place. 'Information to support critical success factors is, by definition, decision support information. It's packaged to support existing decisions and existing activities. It falls under the heading of doing what we do better, as opposed to a revolutionary approach to the way we do business. But I can't identify these new approaches, let alone achieve them. I believe the line manager must do this. Phase one won't just provide decision support. My real plan is that these new information systems will help to create ideas as trends are identified, hidden correlations and connections are exposed, and IT familiarity prompts innovative thinking. When that happens we'll be moving into stage two. We can't discuss this at present because of the culture gap. My role is to provide the IT and create the IS (information systems) that use it. I've got to do this at present. There's no one else. But what's on the hidden agenda is to move IS out to the users. Only IT should be centralized in the long run. The line managers must move the business into the information revolution themselves. My job is just to make it a possible and a friendly thing to do.'

The cases recorded above seem quite innocent. If there was deception, it was done for the best intentions, and always in the company's interests. In fact there was no deception, merely the failure to agree on the real IT objectives.

Well, we all have hidden agendas at various times. Five things make this practice in IT remarkable however:

1   IT directors don't have hidden agendas at various times, they have them all the time.
2   They involve large investments and the consequences always have fundamental effects on the company.
3   Because the overt objectives for computer systems are frequently not the real ones, there are either no performance measures, or wrong ones for checking if the investment was well spent.
4   All examples of hidden agendas seem to be about the IT director's perception of the need to build IT infrastructures, and the difficulty of providing measured justifications for the investment required – in terms of objectives his colleagues understand and support.
5   All the literature on IT ignores the need to have recourse to hidden agendas. It appears to encourage the belief that if the real results of any investment in IT are worthwhile, then once unearthed, cleaned up and made thoroughly visible, they will be immediately acceptable to the company's decision makers, either because of

66 The easy thing to do would be the efficiency job, solve the day-to-day problems and so on. That's what I was appointed for. But slowly I'm changing my role **99**

measurable improvements to the bottom line, or because they are obviously good things to have.

80% OF THE WORLD'S IT SPEND IS JUSTIFIED BY AN OFFICIAL SET OF OBJECTIVES WHOSE ESTIMATED NET BENEFITS ARE KNOWN TO ERR ON THE OPTIMISTIC SIDE, WHICH ARE OFTEN NOT ACHIEVED, AND WHICH THE IT DIRECTOR DOES NOT BELIEVE ARE THE MAIN REASONS FOR THE INVESTMENT.

Part 3

THE MAJOR CONCERNS

66 Let me talk about the IT issues. Issues aren't like problems. Problems can be solved, but issues just keep on bubbling away beneath the surface 99

66 These are the vital things, things for which we have no answers:

- Managing change that we can't see in advance, and caused by a technology that management doesn't understand
- Rationalizing the role of the centre when the technology offers ever increasing self-sufficiency to the individual
- Creating automated systems whose total complexity is beyond our grasp
- Justifying investment in a technology whose benefits we can't measure 99

Chapter 4

Culture gap

66 When information was word of mouth, a handwritten note, books and newspapers, we took it all for granted. It is the new technology, which processes information, that is causing the cultural revolution. It takes things out of our hands. That's worrying enough. What makes it worse, it keeps us in touch with everything – although there's less and less we can do about it. There's one compensation though. Global communication. It enables us to complain about living with computers to anyone, anywhere and at any time 99

Section 1
The evidence

" The users say we can do all this on a PC. The techies say no you can't, there are bigger, wider issues which you can't understand. This is the culture gap: they're both trying to get in on the same game. The IT department's defence is to say it's all too complex for you. But the user is tired of hearing us say we can't deliver "

" What I found was this great void, where the IT techies would talk a lot of gobbledegook, and then say it'll be a four-year project. All the techies could do was go round at the lowest possible level and say: What systems do you need? Never did it come from the top down. No one ever said: This is what we need to run our business "

In Figure 3.5 of the last chapter, IT directors' problems were ranked according to what they felt to be their main difficulty. It showed that the major constraint on further progress was neither technical nor managerial. Nor was it a problem of resources. It was one of understanding.

> 47% OF IT DIRECTORS STATED THEIR MAIN PROBLEM WAS THE CULTURE GAP EXISTING BETWEEN IT AND BUSINESS PROFESSIONALS.

The nearest rival problem (integrating IT with imprecise corporate objectives) trailed the so-called culture gap problem by five percentage points. It was a startling admission. But, stated so baldly, it was hard to get a handle on what the culture gap problem really was. It begged a lot of questions. Chief among them was: What does culture gap really mean?

A further survey was conducted therefore, specifically to probe the cause and effects of the gap, and what were the two cultures that were being separated. This survey provided dramatic confirmation of the problem.

> 56% OF IT DIRECTORS BELIEVE THE CULTURE GAP IS LOSING OR SERIOUSLY DELAYING IT OPPORTUNITIES FOR THEIR COMPANY TO GAIN COMPETITIVE EDGE.

On a first analysis, the culture gap seems to be one of understanding. And it all seems to be weighted on the side of the technicians; who perceive the way the world is going, who see so clearly what is best for us, and who sigh each day 'if only the user could understand'.

There is an attempt to blame the manufacturers for over-praising their product, as though the rule of Caveat Emptor should in some way be suspended in the case of computer salesmen.

And there is some condescending acknowledgement that we technicians, blessed with the truth, are yet to blame – we have failed to explain, we are trying in the wrong ways, and so on. And so on.

To be fair, there are some who do not feel it is such a problem. Some five percent of IT directors questioned on the subject expressed this view. They either didn't believe it presented a major difficulty, or stated they'd solved it.

Another interesting group (eight percent) dismissed the problem to some extent, saying that, while their company experienced a culture gap, it was normal that professionals in any field knew more about their subject than the layman. That was why they were there.

It is the consideration of this view – and confronting it with the fact that, after thirty years of applying the new information technology in business, an overwhelming majority of companies who live happily enough with accountants, lawyers, plumbers and the canteen manager, have been unable to absorb either the computer or the computer professionals into their culture – that suggests there is something more to this gap than just not understanding the IT jargon.

A clue to what this might be is suggested by the comment 'Their knowledge threatens mine' made by one user manager.

And by the cry of one IT director: 'No one would believe the continual frustration this job entails'.

So deep, so ingrained, is the culture gap in the opinion of many, that only time will eradicate it. It is a generation gap, they claim. The young understand the information revolution. They accept the shift from the material, to its electronic representation. More than that, they welcome it. It suits today's over-populated, over-producing planet.

Most important, they have nothing; no career, no hard-won experience nor tricks of the trade to lose. Figure 4.1 shows that over a quarter of IT directors believe that despite training, awareness programs and

66 The culture gap is caused by unrealistic user expectations fuelled by misleading IT advertising **99**

66 IT management need to explain terms and issues as simply as possible and not try to blind line management with jargon **99**

66 The culture gap is not really a significant problem to me today. Regular senior level contact on IT matters throughout the company has largely solved it **99**

66 I don't acknowledge that this culture gap is greater or more significant in the case of IT than in the case of any other specialist function in a business; such as finance, engineering or marketing **99**

66 It's no worse than the culture gap between other professionals like accountants and lawyers who have learned to work successfully as part of a top management team **99**

" Culture changes take time. The business culture reflects the past. IT culture is a precursor, however. In the short-term, IT must bend to the business culture. It's in our recruitment that we must take account of future needs "

" The transition to computer systems and learning to use the management information they provide is traumatic for the manager who has been with the company for a long time. This is when he becomes aware of the culture gap, and will try to avoid IT because he doesn't feel confident about it "

example, the current generation of managers will never fully accept the role of information technology in their work, and pin their hopes on the new people who will be doing their jobs in five and more years' time.

The majority, however, are unhappy with the waiting game.

Q: How long will the culture gap be a significant problem?

Figure 4.1 Time as the healer

"THERE IS STILL THE ERRONEOUS BELIEF THAT COMPUTERS ARE FOR THE YOUNG. SENIOR MANAGEMENT IS HOPING THEIR JUNIOR STAFF WILL SOLVE ALL THEIR IT PROBLEMS."

Section 2
How much change can we take?

66 Automating all the routine work, integrating all our control and communications systems, running the business through decision support systems at every level – it's a massive job. We just don't have enough change agents to make it happen 99

66 The problem is not with junior staff. It lies mostly with senior executives and with middle managers in user areas, who are older and less likely to change 99

One of the main causes of the culture gap is change. IT cannot be taken in isolation. Each dose involves the recipient in changing their behaviour. By definition, a machine is going to do part of your job, control is going to be exercised in a different way.

To this extent, culture gap is a euphemism for threat. The gap exists, because those comfortable with the existing culture do not want it changed.

Changing someone's job, responsibility, prestige: these things are key to IT resistance. Astonishingly, many IT professionals are still surprised that they are not welcomed with open arms; and believe they would be, if only the user understood. It is however, because he understands only too well that enthusiastic IT evangelists encounter such wooden hostility.

In addition to behavioral change, a number of fundamental conceptual changes are also demanded by the application of IT:

The human resources division of a multinational group, operating in food production, distribution and in hotel chains, analyzed the effects of automation by asking fifty of its senior managers what they perceived to be its most fundamental effects. Seven factors were identified:

1) **Power separated from responsibility**
   Many complained that whilst they retained responsibility for the results of their unit, their power to achieve them was diminished as more and more of their control systems were taken out of their hands and transferred onto the computer.

66 What I do affects what everyone else does. It cuts into empires, work patterns, how decisions are taken, even the ownership of information. Everyone resists it. I was appointed because of previous failures. But as I succeed, so shall I be assassinated 99

Case

2) **Boundaries redrawn**

Ubiquitous information networks render hierarchical line and command structures irrelevant. Matrix structures attempting to reconcile the interrelation of line and support functions have become inadequate. IT allows the true complexity of control interrelationships to be mirrored. This encourages the formation of temporary formal, or sometimes informal, groupings to meet objectives, and then to disperse. Job descriptions are becoming vague. Departmental boundaries are softening. Project management is becoming the order of the day.

3) **Growth no longer equals more staff**

Growth is achieved not by increasing the number employed, or the resources owned, but by enlarging the sphere of control or influence. Mergers, and less formal relationships, achieved through EDI, remove whole layers of management and yet increase total turnover and, more important, the security of the links in the value chain.

4) **Work is enjoyment**

Automation has removed the need for hard physical labour, for repetitious, boring work, and even the need to work at all. It has allowed us to focus on the true nature of work as a social activity. The provision of IT facilities at work for every member of staff to feel they participate in the information age is becoming a necessity.

5) **Self-control replaces authority**

Once individuals are given access to all the information needed to achieve their objectives, and know that others have information about their performance, they become motivated to achieve without frequent supervisory contact.

6) **Change becomes the priority**

IT fails to match human performance on any task which has been designed to suit the capabilities of human beings. Its benefits only appear when we do something new, or in a new way. This puts a penalty on stability and a premium on change.

7) **Distance no longer limits organization size**

Organizations are limited in size by their ability to communicate effectively with their staff, their machines, their suppliers and their customers. IT has virtually removed this limitation as a valid constraint in practice.

One of the effects of the culture gap is to encourage the resistance to change, and for firms to take their computer medicine in such palatable doses as require little or no new behaviour or thinking on the part of the patient.

ONE IN FOUR IT DIRECTORS ADMIT THE CULTURE GAP HAS
RESULTED IN WRONG OR ILL-CONCEIVED SYSTEMS.

ONE IN FIVE SAY IT HAS FORCED THEM TO CONCENTRATE
ON CHEAP SOLUTIONS AND COST CUTTING.

89% STATE THEY ARE ENCOURAGED TO AUTOMATE EXISTING
SYSTEMS RATHER THAN CONSIDER NEW WAYS OF DOING
BUSINESS.

Section 3
Attitudes

❝It's easy to say: culture gap. Heads nod wisely. But what does it mean? Distance becoming unimportant, working at home, the global village? These are side effects. The new culture will arrive when the users accept competition is only about information, and the technicians accept that information is all about competition❞

❝I can't deliver what I want to deliver unless I get the executive awareness bit right. They can see the firm's product. And they can see that distribution is getting it there, marketing is selling it and finance is counting the numbers. But what we do in IT is a mystery, an irrelevance. What managers don't see is that they're only as good as their information❞

❝ I'd like to see a high proportion of IT directors with no IT background. Get the culture gap out of the business, and into the IT department ❞

❝ The board is finding it difficult to move from an intellectual to an active position of support ❞

❝ They're often simple things. Customer

The culture gap is more than a lack of IT understanding. It is more than the fact that its application involves resistance: resistance to change and resistance because of a real or perceived threat. One of the main causes is a fundamental difference in attitudes between the users and the IT professionals.

Many feel that, if attitudes differ, it is up to the IT department to adjust, that the business is what is important, and no computer system should be allowed to cause disruptive cultural problems there.

Others admit to what is surely to be expected when confronted with change of a fundamental nature. There are two stages of perception, they say. It is one thing to accept that something is theoretically right. It is quite another to give it the green light and go for it in practice. Most of senior management has moved to the first stage and accept the business novelty that IT could introduce. But few are prepared to lead the revolution.

There are certain specific attitude problems which contribute to the culture gap. On the user side (if there is a gap, then we have to admit there are two sides) one of the most important concerns the ownership of information.

A legacy from the traditional way of collecting and storing data (manual recording and filing) is the concept of the personal ownership of information. It is thought of as a possession. If you work for something and acquire it as a result of your own labour, you own it. So it is with information. We feel we own what we know. There is a sense of prestige: 'I know something you don't know'. But knowledge is power and is worth money. To let it go is to relinquish power, to dilute its value. To release control over it is to risk its misuse, its corruption, its loss.

IT challenges this concept. It works on the premise that the corporation owns the information, not the individual or department that collects it. And it makes it available according to corporate permission, and not as a personal favour.

It is extremely difficult to change established attitudes in this area. Departments needing the same information frequently duplicate it, develop it and jealously guard what they have developed.

In the early days of computing, when data was first stored in a central database, users would commonly continue to maintain their own duplicate files, and set more store by their own lists than the computer's. This was understandable: they took more care to keep their own lists accurate. They did not trust the computer.

Today, computers are more trustworthy. But the attitude dies hard. The departmental attitude to information is held by many to be the biggest barrier to building the IT infrastructures that twenty first century survival strategies are beginning to demand.

The paradox is that while our proprietorial attitude to information clearly demonstrates that we all recognize the value of information, no one is prepared to put a figure on it. From an investment justification point of view, we write it off as an intangible benefit of computer systems. The information itself has no value, we say. Its only value is the use someone makes of it.

The problem with this attitude is that it makes the expensive IT system needed to collect, store and dispense the information impossible to justify on a forecast return for money basis.

If one side of the information ownership coin is that you own the information you spend money collecting, then the other is that you don't spend money collecting information that you don't need.

But it is fundamental to building an IT infrastructure that the information stored there is for the corporate good. Frequently the most efficient way to collect it will be to use a department which has no use for it. Traditional cost/benefit attitudes create problems in this connection, not only in justifying the costs, but also in ascribing responsibility for its collection and maintenance if it is a new task, and not just a by-product of some existing collection process.

addresses are held in ten or twenty places. In at least five or six different representations. And you try to get anyone to accept a standard format! Or let someone else have their address list! **99**

66 I'm having great difficulty in proving that information systems implemented to gain competitive edge are actually improving the bottom line **99**

66 Once you start to build a common database, the culture gap really starts to show. Department A can use some information for the corporate good. Only department B can collect it, however. This adds to B's costs, and for no direct return. B doesn't like this. When they have to go cap in hand to department C to collect it because it was always assumed C owned it, they like it even less "

" I believe the key reason for the culture gap is that both parties do not understand the role of the other. IT staff fail to see the ultimate responsibility of the user to run the business: the users fail to understand many of the technical responsibilities in IT necessary to provide a secure and acceptable service "

" It's astonishing that, in a company which is all about selling technology, our managers are so anti it. Even though they're mostly engineers. They practice management as an art form. Sure it requires some flair. But there really is no feeling that much of the administration control systems could be engineered just like any other control system "

" The biggest IT management mystery of all, is how a technology, which has so consistently failed to deliver, remains so consistently successful with its pleas for further funding "

" It is interesting to note that, when I

It is a firmly established attitude that different functions have inherent roles in organizations, that these roles are of two types: line and support, and that IT is a support function. This attitude does not, in itself, contribute to the culture gap; since it seems to be held equally by both users and IT staff. But it is not applied equally.

IT staff constantly shelter behind it to defend their escalating costs to achieve technical excellence, and to avoid responsibility for getting benefits.

The users, and particularly top management however, are prone to ask for value for money. But they cannot have their cake and eat it. Whilst the line/support attitude persists, IT contribution to the bottom line is clearly impossible. There is no value in a support function per se – only in the use a line department makes of the services it provides.

An attitude which greatly contributes to the culture gap is that management are basically against technology when it comes to using it in their own field. Until the advent of the electronic computer, management was about judgement and motivation. Judgement was exercised intuitively, and often brilliantly, based on unformulated experience. Motivation, similarly, relied on personal qualities: of charisma and of persuasion.

It is an entirely new concept that management can be partly exercised by a machine, that routine administration can be automated. Attitudes change slowly. And the change process is inhibited in two ways.

Firstly, by fear. 'Everyone is down on what they're not up on', as one US IT executive put it. What more natural than that any manager who doesn't understand IT, and this must include ninety percent, should be afraid of it to some extent.

Secondly, by cynicism. By a frank disbelief that IT will work, produce benefits, be up and running on time, be free of serious errors and keep within budgeted costs. The IT department's past performance, unfortunately, does little to dispel this attitude. Even today, there are enough disasters: cost escalations, missed deadlines, performance shortcomings, systems which simply do not work as promised – to provide ammunition for any senior manager who wishes to cast doubt on plans for further automation.

Attitude problems are not all in the user departments. The technicians are notorious for their inclination to pursue, some might say indulge, technical objectives at the expense of the business.

No one would deny the professional pride a system analyst or programmer takes in performing feats of wizardry on the computer. Nor the pride they take in working with the latest equipment. In this respect they are no different from any other profession.

In every other profession it is controlled within practical and economic bounds by the price the client is prepared to pay and his satisfaction with the work done. Most of the IT profession however, do not practice as professionals in this sense, working under contract for clients. They are employees of the business. There is no contractual control exercised on professional self-indulgence therefore.

Many IT staff put the business interests first. But we do well to remember that the business is not their first love. They joined to work on computers, and it would not be surprising if, consciously or subconsciously, they got a kick out of standing them on their heads.

There is a noticeable attitude on the part of IT staff to prefer and to discuss hard rather than soft solutions. By hard, we mean definitive procedures, with no room for discretion. This is because these are the only procedures a computer can carry out, and they are motivated and used to thinking in this way.

Management, on the other hand, deal with people, and people do not respond well to detailed prescription. They prefer some latitude. Management also have to contend with moving targets and instinctively shun detailed planning. At the detailed level, plans may quickly become obsolete. Management deal in soft possibilities, not hard certainties.

We discussed earlier the attitude of users to value for money from their IT investment: they want it, yet they are shy of accepting they are responsible for it. IT people are equally shy in this respect. By and large, they are pretty clear that their job is to provide systems for the users, systems which the users ask for, specify, sign for and make of what they can.

Between the pair of them, user and IT professional, if they both have their way, it seems that responsibility for business results disappears somewhere down the culture gap.

> ONLY 7% OF IT DIRECTORS ADMIT TO BEING RESPONSIBLE FOR THE PAYOFF FROM THE IT INVESTMENT.

These attitude problems are at the root of the culture gap. By way of summary, Figure 4.2 (see p. 121) sets out a number of polarized concepts; attitudes where the IT department and the users are most distinctly at loggerheads.

It is a consistent moan of IT professionals that the users do not get involved in IT – that the IT department is expected to identify applications, solve problems and implement solutions on its own, presenting the company with bottom line benefits on a plate, all without disturbing a hair on the user's body.

The IT director of a member company in a major US group with diverse interests explained the culture gap as two problems:

asked my staff recently 'Which business are you in?', most said 'The computer industry', as opposed to music or entertainment, which is our business 99

66 IT continues to be focussed more on the technology than the information: its availability and its use to support business objectives 99

66 Don't blame the users. The key problem is the ability of IT staff to communicate on the business level with general management 99

66 Being appointed director is finding a lot of IT people out. They can't stand up to board level operating. They were doing OK at the information systems level, specifying work for computers. But their ability to hold their own and have the business debate was a myth. This is far and away the most crucial function. That's where people really buy in – when they think you understand the business and you're contributing 99

Case

- Senior management is afraid of technology, so they don't get involved in IT decisions early enough. So the company makes technical solutions. And to the wrong problems.
- The users can't get involved in projects at the right level. So projects go askew, and everyone blames the technologists.

'This is not an issue with us!' he hastened to add. 'We've been through all that. I have all IT decentralized now. But I still see it elsewhere in the group. I'm part of the IT audit team. The first thing we look at is the involvement of the non-dp management in the project. This is the 'only and always' cause of failure. We just collapsed a project which was mismanaged at the corporate level. The project was going fine. It was just the wrong project. This lack of user participation has always been a problem. But it's worse today, because today's systems are more important. Take the reservation system we're putting in at . . . . It's the heart of the business. But the marketing executive wasn't involved in it. We put in our report, and they understand *now* that it's their accountability and not the data processing individuals'. So the project's back in focus.'

The culture gap undoubtedly leads to non-participation by the users. It also leads to a somewhat self-righteous and defensive attitude in the IT department, as this case shows. Our research convinced us that the culture gap was a very deep-rooted problem, and of a much more fundamental nature than the simple knowledge gap experienced when dealing with other specialists. IT affects everyone's job.

We recall that, asked to describe his role in a sentence, one IT director replied 'I am a bridge.'

If we were asked to describe, in a word, the effect of the culture gap on IT directors, the answer would certainly be 'Frustration'.

> 66 The most fundamental problem is that business management sees it as IT's job to deliver solutions. They don't understand their role as driving the business changes needed to make the IT element of the solution effective 99

18% OF IT DIRECTORS ARE DENIED THE OPPORTUNITY TO BRAINSTORM IT BUSINESS POTENTIAL WITH TOP MANAGEMENT.

31% SAY BUSINESS PEOPLE HAVE DIFFICULTY UNDERSTANDING AND APPRECIATING THE WORTH OF IT PEOPLE, AND ABSORBING THEM WITHIN THE ORGANIZATION.

A FURTHER 30% SAY BUSINESS PEOPLE HAVE DIFFICULTY TRUSTING IT STAFF.

COMPARE AND CONTRAST

	IT dept.	vs.	users

"The most powerful directors have got themselves in their position because they're very good at resolving problems. But they won't solve them for tomorrow. Because they rather like problems coming up. If there are no problems coming up, they're not doing their job."

planning — off the cuff

"The culture gap is really a planning gap. Two lines in the corporate plan can become forty thousand lines in a systems spec. The problem is for a user to articulate their needs at the level of detail needed by a systems engineer."

detailed procedures — setting objectives

"The most important thing is achieving a correct balance between renewing the base infrastructure and dealing with the short term, immediate business concerns."

long term view — short term view

"The business calls for bottom line. Will someone tell me how to put a measured value on information?"

intangible benefits — tangible benefits

"The trouble is decentralization of IT has followed the decentralization of the business. That's the wrong driver. The logic of what part of IT should be under user control has nothing to do with politics."

distributed processing — political decentralization

"Most users think that changing a computer system is a question of shouting at it."

rigidity — flexibility

"Have you noticed how an IT man prides himself on his knowledge? He's paid for what he knows. But knowledge doesn't count for much in this business. There the people who matter are those who take responsibility for results."

knowledge — responsibility

"The principle problem is no longer the automation of processes. It is the communication of information between processes where we're screwing it up at present."

integration — autonomy

"IT will remain a relatively small proportion of the total resource until we acknowledge it is the real resource. What does that mean 'information is the real resource?' Hew can grasp that. Only if they do will the chief executive be an IT man, or will they have an IT man as a member of the main board, responsible for results."

information systems are a key resource — information systems play a support role

"I keep coming back to convince them that the return on IT investment is not my problem."

investment based on feasibility — investment based on justification

Figure 4.2
Polarized concepts

Section 4
Overcoming the problem

❝ The culture gap will close on its own in time. But have we got time? The question is what can I do to hurry it along? ❞

Figure 4.3 shows the main methods for overcoming the culture gap adopted by IT directors. Clearly IT directors of the world are not yet ready to make the supreme sacrifice, and, however frustrated, believe it is in the company's interests that they should live to fight another day.

Many pin their hopes on education. General education on IT, for users and top management, is universally condemned as a waste of time however. To be effective, it has to be specifically addressed to a corporate need.

Disenchanted by general education, many have recourse to the submission of papers to senior managers, again addressing specific topics. This may release a lot of the author's frustration, but, to use the vernacular, appears in most cases to be a cop-out. The culture gap cannot begin to be addressed in the popular one-page management summary.

IT directors need to face the fact, however, that papers of any length irritate rather than lubricate user relations.

❝ Our major agent for change is IT strategy Masterclasses structured to bring home to senior directors that there is a problem with both benefits and threats to their business. Generalized IT training for executives is a waste of time and must be focussed to their needs, as they perceive them ❞

Case

It was in the large, oak-panelled, IT director's office, in one of the world's largest multinationals. We were there to discuss the IT director's role, concerns, problems and the ways ahead. We had two hours. He started discussing the culture gap. Suddenly it was eleven. The interview was over. We had discussed nothing else. 'The gap is a mile wide,' he'd said. 'Whatever level you look at, the board, on the shop floor. It's a great gulf.' He had produced 'my efforts over one year' – a massive green folder, full to bursting with sheaves of papers all to do, we were told, with explaining to the users what their role in life is, in relation to using, managing and harnessing computer systems. He had shown us a paper entitled User Participation. 'Didn't have much effect', he said. 'You can see that by the number of papers I've had to put up since.' He waved his hand at the rows of shelves at the side of his desk. Papers, folders, binders, each labelled with its title, and arranged in sections, also labelled, this time with embossed titles fixed on each shelf. The Role of the Board, one said. The Chief Information Officer's

Role, said another. Features and Benefits of Office Automation, User Participation, Technology Leverage and the Nature of IT Benefits. They stretched far beyond his desk, too far to read them all. Finally he said 'There's only one answer to the culture gap. It's education. But you can see . . . ' He waved again at the shelves, and the silent papers stacked along them. 'You can see, it's going to take a long time.'

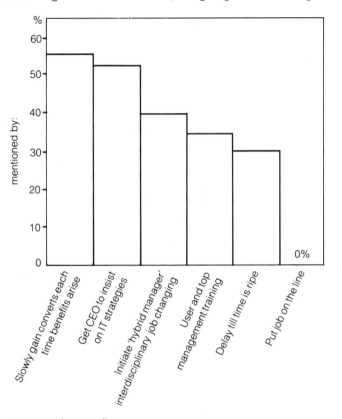

Figure 4.3 Popular remedies

IT history is littered with bandwagons. Wheels off, lying in the ditch, they are there for all to see and wonder over.

The one that is up and rolling at the moment is called The Hybrid Manager. To bridge the culture gap, the theory goes, we need a manager, or preferably all managers, who have experience in both the business and in IT. It must, by definition, be true that when everyone has been brought up in an 'IT in Business' culture, there will be no culture gap. According to many IT directors, this particular bandwagon seems to have rolled obliviously over a couple of red lights. Being actually brought up in a culture is a world away from a retraining course and six months' exposure to the problems. True hybrids, they say, are a generation away.

More important, hybrids on their own will not solve the problem. IT benefits mean doing something new. They mean visionaries, creative

❝ Interdisciplinary job changing is pie in the sky at present, but it's a worthy goal ❞

❝ The hybrid manager bandwagon is ill-conceived and unhelpful, and I know many other IT directors who think likewise. The current campaigns to promote it are out of touch with reality ❞

people. Such people do not grow on trees. Nor can they be forced in a training plus experience greenhouse.

❝ To ask the top man to spend $250 million just on the say so of his IT director, is one hell of a thing to do. But that's what I'm asking ❞

Near the top of the list is the big stick technique. It is perhaps a quibble to note that the stick does not cure the culture gap. It drives IT into the business by ignoring it. The popular big stick is the CEO. If the top man supports an IT project it is likely to take off. In addition to his authority, the chief executive has, by virtue of his position, two important immunities to the culture gap. He is the only person whose job responsibility is not affected by a major IT project. And he is the only person who can truly take a cross-departmental view.

❝ It's the problem with all revolutions. We are being lead by visionaries, not by men who've already been there ❞

The chief executive however is not the only person who can wield the big stick. Any visionary, who is in a position of sufficient authority, can become the necessary instrument of change. As we have seen, most successful cases illustrating business advantage through the imaginative use of IT have their user champion, usually the head of the function which will spearhead the application. Once again, the culture gap is not closed. The visionary is followed, not out of a sense of conviction, but as an act of faith, loyalty and obedience to the leader.

❝ The culture gap doesn't exist here. I am responsible for all operations – finance, manufacturing, distribution, personnel and retail. I'm also responsible for IT ❞

The key point is that the culture gap can be overcome, not cured but overcome, by anyone who has both the responsibility for IT and for achieving business results. This marriage of responsibility closes the gap, as far as that person is concerned. He knows, and is prepared to use, the capability of IT. And he has business improvement objectives. And there is really no reason whatever why that person should not be the IT director.

❝ In an intellectual sense, most managers clearly perceive the potential of IT. But they must also feel good about what IT actually delivers. We need to concentrate on providing friendly and simple solutions to the problems they own and recognize ❞

The most popular solution is virtually to conduct a continual IT exercise – to keep whittling away at the problem in a very practical way, that is, by constantly providing examples of what IT can achieve. Small examples at first. Low cost, quick to implement. And always directed at a problem recognized by, and currently concerning, a senior manager.

'Show them IT can give them what they want. That's the first step,' said one IT director. 'Then, when they're finally listening, show them it can also transform the business.'

> 55% OF IT DIRECTORS STATE THE BUSINESS POTENTIAL OF IT IS NOT APPRECIATED BY TOP MANAGEMENT.
>
> 46% STATE THE BUSINESS IMPLICATIONS OF IT ARE NOT APPRECIATED BY IT STAFF.

Chapter 5

The future of the centralized IT department

❝ People say what holds an organization together is common objectives, an accidental or a conscious commitment, or a need to co-operate. But, at rock bottom, it is a common information system. A moment's thought will suffice to convince that, without communication, co-operation is neither possible, nor even relevant ❞

Section 1
Decentralization and user power

❝I think there is a danger that IT control will be taken from IT specialists and given totally to general management. This will not improve the situation at all – just create a different form of maladministration❞

What is decentralization? When the term is applied to IT, it can mean two entirely different things. There is hardware decentralization, technically known as distributed processing, and there is the decentralization of control.

Hardware decentralization, by itself, means little more than spreading computery around the organization, and around one's suppliers' and customers' organizations. Either octopus-like, with centralized processing and memory, and with sensory input and output tentacles – or, like a daisy chain, with equal, interchangeable nodes, sharing the functional honours as required*. But, in both cases, connected. So that each may still be driven by a centre, no user having independent authority.

The technical problems of distributed processing, especially with interchangeable processors and memories, are very exciting. The only management significance however, is that the responsibility for inputing data to the computer system lies with the user, who feels the pain when he makes a mistake, and has the power to put it right. This balancing of power and responsibility is a fundamental improvement on the remote, centralized input of data enforced by the early, entirely centralized installations.

❝ The new, decentralized units wanted their own kit and their own IT men. It was feelings versus logic ❞

With the decentralization of control however, the users do have a measure of stand-alone authority. A complete measure in some cases. This is of basic organizational and management significance. It is this second aspect of IT decentralization which we shall discuss in this chapter.

Figure 5.1 shows that there was really no alternative to total centralization when computers were first introduced into business.

* Students of management and organization, noticing the change of metaphor from animal to artifact, will sympathize – since few animals, if any, are organized as a circle. They may feel encouraged to ask why?

In the early '60s, the hardware was too expensive for each user to have his own machine. A single machine was purchased, installed centrally and shared. The skills to run it, and to develop systems, were in too short supply, and required too specialized management for the users to do their own thing. And there were no communications to speak of, which would enable the users to connect their desks to this centralized processor.

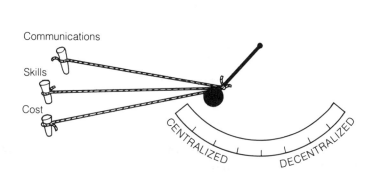

Figure 5.1 The constraints on decentralization

But, during the '70s, these constraints were gradually relaxed. Cheap hardware, especially micros; packaged, off-the-shelf programs; and networks, all freed up the pendulum, artificially held in the centralized position, and allowed it to swing naturally between the two poles of organization structure.

Where will it come to rest? The balance between centralization and decentralization in an organization is always shifting: to satisfy different weightings attached to economies of scale, to the importance of autonomy (cynics say to satisfy the dictates of fashion) or to the simple need for change. So it may turn out to be for IT. But at the present time, with the emphasis on centralization for so long, all the trends point to increased decentralization (Figure 5.2).

In answer to the question 'do you expect the users to have more or less control over IT during the next twelve months?' IT executives have never answered 'less' since 1975. Since it was virtually nil at that time, an increase is not surprising. The swing to user power has been slow

❝ The flavours of decentralization change as the business and the technology changes ❞

but, since 1982, very steady however, and the user controlled IT spend, which by-passes the centralized IT budget, now stands at about a fifth of the total.

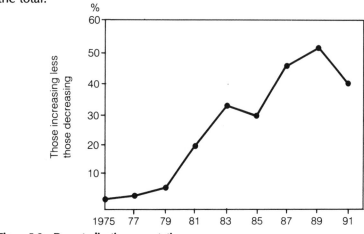

Figure 5.2   Decentralization expectations

It is predicted to rise to a quarter within four years. An interesting breakdown of the trend is shown by the figures showing the discretionary spend (Figure 5.3). The discretionary spend is money that does not have to be spent in order to keep the existing IT investment functioning. It is the spend on new systems. Since it is the current, and not the old, IT applications that are taking computers into the front line of the business, the discretionary spend is arguably the most important from the point of view of computer strategy.

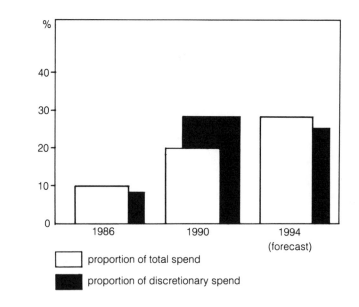

Figure 5.3   The proportion of user-controlled IT

Here, the trend to user power is much more marked, and already accounts for a quarter of the total. This is no more than to be expected. The centre was responsible for the great bulk of the existing investment – and naturally is burdened with its maintenance. It puts the users in a strong position of influence however. In many cases they have green-field sites, and unhindered by the past, can take IT down new directions, and exploit the latest technology, far more easily than can the centre.

By 1994 however, this difference between the user's proportion of the discretionary spend and the total is expected to disappear, for three reasons:

1   Many IT directors are driving hard at the heavy maintenance costs of the old centralized systems, and are replacing them with low maintenance versions.
2   The role of the centre to produce core systems is becoming clearer; these cores will have become a substantial and continuing investment by 1994.
3   By then, the users will be saddled with substantial maintenance costs themselves.

There are, in the main, only two possible types of drivers for the swing to decentralization: technical drivers and business drivers. We have noted that the constraints holding IT artificially in a centralized position were all technical. Since these have now been removed, it is tempting to assume that the current decentralization trend has been led by the new technology.

There seems to be no substance in this however. There is no technological argument which weights the argument in favour of splitting up computers. The economies of scale and the avoidance of duplication always tilt the balance. It is perfectly true that the enormous centralized systems constructed in the past are now proving cumbersome, and impossible to change. But there are ways of building large systems in small modules which overcome these problems.

Despite the implications, in the suppliers' literature, of networks and server/workstation architecture replacing centralized mainframes, the influence of the technology seems to have been only one of an enabler, allowing existing pressures for decentralization to take effect. The pressure for it, the trend to user-controlled IT, was, in the first place, business driven.

Three main business drivers can be identified:

> **❝** It's not an IT issue but an organizational issue. Do you want to run the business through the regions or through the centre? You deploy your IT hardware and systems to mirror the business structure **❞**

1 Decentralization of the business

The large centralized organization philosophy, based on the economies of scale, and the increased effectiveness of large-scale applications of capital on production plant and on marketing, was at its heyday in the '50s. Since then, the human factors of motivation, and the difficulty of controlling these giants, have been paid more attention. Corporate growth has continued to take place, but it has become fashionable to organize large companies as a collection of self-contained business units, run by autonomous managers rewarded according to the results achieved. The pressure on IT to follow suit, and be dispersed among these autonomous units, was intensified in the '80s as central costs rose. The automatic allocation of these costs amongst the local units was resented by managers, who wanted control over their costs.

Case

❝ We broke it up by commodity. Each commodity defined a business **❞**

❝ The computer systems had been designed to serve the company as a whole. We couldn't access the database to provide the detailed information the new business units wanted. It meant more than splitting up the systems. It meant a rewrite **❞**

❝ There was always user dissatisfaction. But it was just moaning until we decentralized. Then the users got teeth **❞**

In 1980, a major European chemical and engineering company considered how best to break up the business into more manageable units. They considered combining those who shared raw materials, or who shared common production technologies, or who shared common marketing strategies or who shared common customers. In the end they decided the break-up should be according to product. IT was retained as a centralized function shared by the product divisions. After eight years, pressure was exerted by the business unit heads, and IT responsibility was decentralized to them. There were five main reasons:

● Concern about the level of corporate costs.
● Concern to give each business control over the whole of its value chain, and to hold it responsible for results with complete accountability.
● A further move away from the old command and control organization structure, and towards an accountable-for-objectives culture.
● A recognition that energies were better directed to dealing with the outside world rather than internal administration.
● Dissatisfaction with the central system, which had been designed to process information by customer, and was unable to produce management information required by the new business units, which were organized by product.

2 User dissatisfaction with the centralized IT service

The we/they atmosphere that grew up during the first twenty years of computing in business, with technicians accused of professional self-indulgence, delays in systems development leading to programming backlogs of two and more years, and user dissatisfaction with compulsory doses of automation, often worsening rather than improving business performance, finds a new voice when the business decentralizes. Firstly, the users have more power, and must be listened to. Secondly, they have a belief that they can do it better, and autonomy encourages them to try. Thirdly, once decentralized, they soon cease to receive IT services for free. Chargeback systems are introduced, and complaints about the cost soon result.

3 *IT department cost reduction drives*
Irrespective of any move towards decentralization, there has, as we have seen, been a widespread business drive since the 1985 Watershed, to reduce the central costs of IT. Many IT directors stated quite openly that cost containment and cost reduction policies provide a strong incentive to decentralize; offloading onto the users enables them to cut the centralized budget. Whether this reduces the overall spend on IT is highly questionable – but the question isn't raised while the users are happy to take over control.

66 It's no cheaper to decentralize. But once you decentralize IT, you lose sight of the costs. So it looks like a saving 99

> THE PROPORTION OF IT SPEND THAT IS UNDER USER CONTROL IS RISING STEADILY AT THE RATE OF TWO AND A HALF PER CENT EACH YEAR.

Section 2
The rationale of an IT centre

❝ The major issue today is at Chief Executive level, and is about the relationship between IT and the core business ❞

In the face of this steady swing to decentralization, and the admission that IT was only centralized in the beginning because there was no option, the question has to be asked: Where will it end? Will the trend take us to a position of 100% user control of IT? What is the future of the centralized IT department – or of any centralized IT role?

There may be a variety of short-term roles: running down the present centralized systems, for example, which could take many years. And training the users. But, ultimately there is only one justification for a continuing centralized function. And that is co-ordination. These are the fundamental questions:

- If we allow the separate divisions in the company to design and run their own IT systems, is there some corporate need which will not be satisfied?

Case

A multinational oil company recognized that its policy-making and behaviour on environmental issues was a corporate function. The decentralized systems would not process or produce the information required however, and a central system was designed. Following this, centralized systems were then designed to mirror all corporate functions – human resources administration, and public relations, for example.

- Will they talk to each other?

Case

A US company, manufacturing paper and paper-based products, recognized the need for an inter-department electronic mail system, and an executive information system to monitor each department's performance at board level. The separately designed departmental systems could not be connected however, and had to be rewritten according to centrally imposed standards.

- Will they produce something in the corporate interest which is not necessarily in the department's interest?

A bank identified the need to collect information at branch level which was only needed by the corporate marketing function.

Case

- Will they share information for the corporate good?

A manufacturing company found that each of its divisions had installed a separate product design and assembly system, even though many sub-assemblies and parts were common to all divisions. When they proposed a common procurement and design system, it was resisted on the grounds of loss of control by the divisional directors.

Case

- Will they optimize the return from their IT investment, make sensible investments and develop and run their systems successfully?

A local government department, given autonomy, by-passed the IT centre and installed its own computer. It failed to realize however, that it could have saved 40% of its systems development costs by using a different programming language, and that its hardware was at the top of its range and could not be easily expanded to accommodate further systems. Later, the department was forever being dug out of trouble by the centre because of badly designed systems.

Case

Co-ordination comes in two modes: passive and active.

Examples of passive co-ordination are setting IT policy, setting standards and planning. Figure 5.4 shows that these passive roles scored highest when IT directors were asked to predict what their roles would be in five and ten years' time.

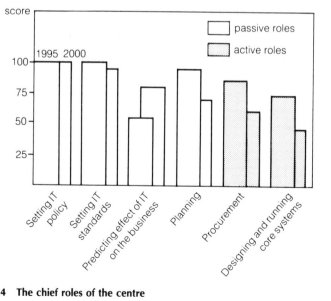

Figure 5.4 The chief roles of the centre

66 If I impose a policy, and it's not accepted, there's no point. So either I get consensus, or it has to be imposed by the chief executive **99**

Policy setting scored highest of all. Closely followed by setting standards, which form the teeth in most policy statements: This is what we shall do, followed by This is how we shall do it.

The distinction between imposed and recommended standards was frequently made. Imposed standards create difficulties for many IT directors when they confine themselves to passive roles. Most have no authority to impose them.

Once again, the importance of the chief executive's role stands out. Implementing standards will almost always be an additional cost, effort and inconvenience to the autonomous department building its own computer systems. The CEO is the only person who can insist they sub-optimize in the interests of the company.

Examples of policy concern which hardware to buy, which programming languages to use, which productivity aids to use and so on. Recent corporate concern however, about the safety of computer systems has raised the issue of security to the top of the list of policy and standards areas for many companies.

> 7% OF COMPANIES NOW ADMIT TO 'MAJOR' OR 'CRIPPLING' LOSSES RESULTING FROM BREACHES OF SECURITY.

Case

A major European manufacturing group identified the security of its information systems as posing one of the biggest threats to its activities. Four areas were identified: system breakdown, error, fraud and loss of information. The IT director commented 'The risk has got greater. We depend more on IT today. And networks, open systems mainly, have increased our vulnerability. It's an internal and an external threat. The technology for penetration is so available. The fear is major fraud. But breakdown is worse in practice. There is plenty we could do. My problem in setting standards is how much to spend, what burdens and constraints to impose on the local systems developers. And what to do if they don't implement them.'

Planning scores third in 1995. While planning is largely technology based – what IT architectures to build and so on – it remains firmly in the passive category.

A move towards a more active role is apparent when planning concerns what IT applications to implement, especially when these decisions are based on predictions of the changing ways of doing business brought about by IT. The whole way the company operates is affected by this role.

One of the most interesting findings, illustrated in Figure 5.4, is the increased emphasis IT directors place on their job to predict the effect of IT on business strategy, comparing their forecast for 1995 (when it barely rates above a fifty per cent score) with the eighty per cent in AD 2000.

More interesting, certainly more dramatic, are the active roles played by the centre.

66 Nothing comes through the door without my approval **99**

Authorizing all purchases of hardware and software comes top of the list in this area. Despite the current talk about internationally agreed standards, which will ensure all machines can talk to each other, and any program will run on any machine, there is frank disbelief in this nirvana by most IT directors, who prefer the more pragmatic approach of censoring what is bought and restricting purchases to within proven compatibility ranges.

> 58% OF IT DIRECTORS BELIEVE IT WILL BE MORE THAN TEN YEARS BEFORE TRUE COMPATIBILITY STANDARDS ARE AGREED AND ADOPTED BY SUPPLIERS.
>
> 38% BELIEVE IT WILL NEVER HAPPEN.

Much more significant, however, is the central activity of designing, building and operating core systems. In future years, history may show that the distinction made between a core system and an application is the most significant new thought to emerge in computing since the machine itself was invented.

66 My role is to identify the commonality in systems **99**

The point has already been made that, for the first twenty-five years of the information revolution, IT departments concentrated on building complete systems to perform isolated applications. Stock control applications for example; order processing, customer accounting, the general ledger and the payroll; each built separately.

Around 1985, a more general recognition became apparent that two parts to an IT system could be identified: a core system, which took on board the basic data flowing into the organization, and applications, which each made various uses of this data, and produced useful outputs. The core was common. It was used subsequently by many applications.

This recognition involved the perception that there were advantages in developing the core system separately from the applications.

The core systems (there may be more than one) comprise the basic, high volume, data capture jobs that record the basic transactions that the company has with its customers and suppliers – orders and deliveries, or cheques and paying-in slips for example. They also comprise the indexing and updating of databases which store this information. And they include the communications IT infrastructure which connects all the hardware in the company, and in other contactable organizations, together.

If cores are built separately, the following advantages are secured:

1 *Division of labour*
Core systems exploit the available technology, especially communications technology. They process high volumes of data, and efficient, often optimal, processing speeds are required. They involve database design and access path design. For these reasons, they demand a high level of programming skills for their construction.

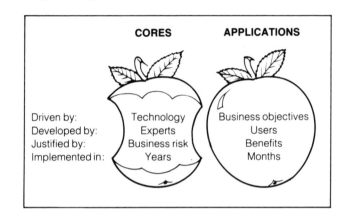

Figure 5.5 Core systems versus applications

Once the core is in place, the skilled work is done. Applications often involve little more than accessing an existing database, and formatting the information required. Easy-to-use fourth generation languages can be employed, since efficient processing is no longer of the essence. Lower skilled, and less experienced, programmers can be used, supervised by the users; sometimes the users themselves can write the application programs.

2 *Timescales*
Designing the core system is difficult; constructing it is also difficult and involves a large amount of programming. It takes the sort of timescale we have become used to in large computer projects; of the order of three years, for example, would not be uncommon – though a core system can, of course, be constructed in small, easier-to-manage modules.

Again, once the core is in place, hanging applications onto it is a relatively quick job. Using fourth generation languages, months, sometimes only days, are required. Applications can be constructed in time to meet the short-term objectives of the business.

3 *Co-ordination*
After some experience of decentralization, it becomes apparent that

❝ It's interesting how the way we portray the

there are no such things as stand-alone applications. All applications are linked in some way, all have some part in common, and require to use a common facility.

We have said that the only true role of the centre is to co-ordinate decentralized systems so that they can talk to each other, share facilities and supply corporate information. Setting policies and standards goes some way towards meeting this objective. Being passive roles however, they do not always succeed. But if the centre lays down a core system, the separate decentralized applications are automatically co-ordinated.

Fortunately (or was it clever anticipation of demand?) the technology, enabling the core systems approach to be implemented, arrived just in time.

computer has changed. We used to draw it, large, at the top of the page – with lines going down to tiny terminals. Sometimes we sat tiny users in front of them. Often we didn't bother. Now, the concept of the macho computer has gone. The users are at the top of the page with their screens. And lines stretch down to the computer, somewhere at the bottom **99**

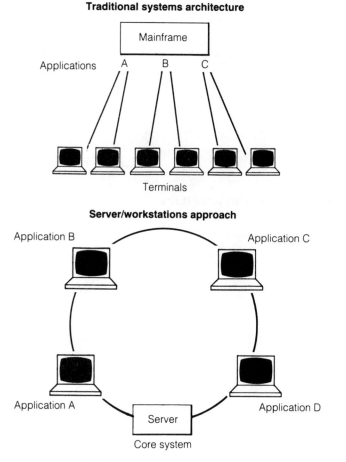

Figure 5.6   The server/workstation strategy

Today, cheaper computers, and improved communications networks, enable much of the processing to be done by local machines linked to a core system, which resides on a computer known as a server. The mainframe is dead, has become a popular cry.

It is not that the need for large machines has died. Core systems will always stimulate a need for powerful computers with large information storage capacity. It is the mainframe concept which has died: a concept of numerous, separate applications, processed centrally.

66 The network is the computer **99**

66 Running an IT infrastructure is the only centralized function **99**

The core system approach provides the rationale for a computing centre. It answers the question 'how much should we decentralize?' If there is any need for the users to communicate and to share information, if there is any need to monitor the business performance of decentralized units and to take corporate action in any sphere, then there is a need for a core IT system. And the responsibility for specifying its functions, designing it and running it is a central one.

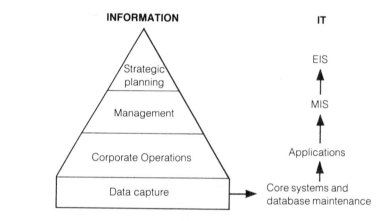

Figure 5.7 Information layers versus IT layers

The fact that IT directors score down its importance by the year 2000 shows that this novel thinking will be old hat by then – and accepted as the norm.

66 In the old days, it was always bottom up. Never from the top down **99**

One director illustrated the need for core systems with the diagram, reproduced in Figure 5.7, showing three layers of information.

Information is needed to drive the company's routine operations, to manage and keep them on course and to plan new strategies. Operating information is about an application. Management information is about a business unit. Strategic information concerns many applications and many business units.

If IT is organized around applications, data gets fed in at the operations level and is not available to support the changing objectives of the business units, and the strategic thinking of the company. The data needs to be stored at the corporate level. It can then be drawn off as required.

THE SPEND ON DEVELOPING AND RUNNING THE
COMPANY'S CORE SYSTEMS IS ESTIMATED TO BE 74% OF THE
TOTAL IT BILL.

BY THE YEAR 2000, NO IT DIRECTORS BELIEVE DESIGNING OR
RUNNING SEPARATE APPLICATIONS WILL ANY LONGER BE A
SIGNIFICANT ROLE OF THE CENTRALIZED IT DEPARTMENT.

OVER THREE QUARTERS PREDICT THEIR MAIN ROLE WILL
SHIFT FROM RUNNING OPERATIONS TO FORECASTING AND
STRATEGIC PLANNING.

Section 3
The problems and processes of decentralization

❝ Taken to extremes, decentralization will always lead to short-term strategies ❞

❝ It's the ownership of data that's the key problem. If people are proprietorial about it, we lose it as a corporate resource. But if no one owns it, it doesn't get collected ❞

❝ What we've been doing over the last five years, since we decentralized, has been determined by a business function. This leads to systems, hopefully packages, installed for their functional fit. And the users have bought whatever hardware goes with this software. So driving IT at the business unit level leads to the satisfaction of local needs, as perceived by businessmen, hoping there's a package. We end up with diversity ❞

Case

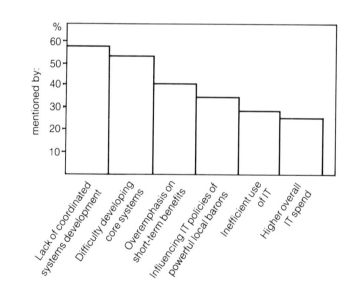

Figure 5.8   The main problems of decentralization

The major problem invoked by decentralizing IT is the lack of natural co-ordination in developing the company's systems, and the difficulty of achieving it subsequently. It is always quicker and cheaper to go for a specific objective, and ignore the interconnections and relationship that the required information has with other functions and needs. These relationships are not always evident anyway – often the need for interconnecting systems only arises after the first system has been built.

A major Japanese conglomerate had seven factories, and each had developed its own information systems. In 1988, they faced a crisis in two areas – they were no longer able to control the company at corporate level, and they were faced with the problem of losing substantial business, since they could not co-operate with the 'just-in-time' systems being installed by their major customers. Since there was no effective centralized IT function, and the decentralized systems had each been installed by separate outside contractors, they called in consultants. A member of the consultancy commented 'The lack of co-ordination has caused problems of inefficiency – the total costs of IT are far greater than they need be – and problems of interfacing. Management cannot get correct figures about what is happening, because the separate information systems cannot be interlinked, and the individual items of information, although called the same in each company, mean different things. Even worse, we cannot present a common file of information to our suppliers, and thus link into their EDI systems, because each supplier deals with many of our factories, and these factories have no common system.'

66 They did it themselves. At half the cost, and in half the time. Later, they needed their system to talk to the rest of the company. It had to be rewritten. At twice the cost, and in double the time. It was a good exercise – there was no other way the company could have learned this lesson 99

Case

66 My main problem is to take business-led divergence, and lead it back, not into convergence, but into non-divergence 99

Following the redesign of the core system in a building society, the arrears department was left with the possession of two redundant workstations. Two members of their staff had some experience with fourth generation languages, and the department decided to build their own systems. They were pleased with the speed they had produced results, having by-passed the queue waiting for the centre to write programs. 'They hadn't followed our open systems standards however,' commented the IT director. 'When they tried to integrate with the payments system infrastructure, they fell flat on their faces. They'd produced a bubble on the side, and it became a cul-de-sac. They couldn't move it forward.'

In addition to co-ordination problems, both of the above cases illustrate the efficiency, and increased cost, problems that go-it-alone users can cause. The technical pull to the centre is justified by the economies of scale, and the expertise available there. These problems appear in the top six in Figure 5.8. They score low mentions, however. There is recognition that the motivational gains achieved by a measure of controlled decentralization can be worth the extra cost.

Close behind the co-ordination problem were the problems encountered with its most effective solution: building core systems. Building core systems involves three main difficulties:

1 *Specifying the requirements*
The core enables subsequent applications to be implemented. Since

many of these applications are for the future, their detailed require-ments are not known, and have to be guessed. What sort of core system do we need to support the business in five and ten years' time? And what is common, or should be dealt with at corporate level, and what should be left to our decentralized systems?

2   *Collecting the data*
The core is run by the centre, but the data arrives locally. It has to be collected locally, often by departments who do not themselves need it, or who, having gone to the expense of collecting it, feel they own it.

3   *Justifying the expense*
Since the core produces no benefits (the benefits come subsequently from the applications) these infrastructures are laid down largely as an act of faith, or, to use the current euphemism, as a busi-ness risk.

Case

A major US construction company attempted to build a core system, and identified all the data sources needed to support their business objectives. They failed to construct a complete database in their first attempt however, because of the difficulty of setting up and justifying all the data collection systems required. 'We're having to build in two stages,' said the IT director. 'We're concentrating on production first, because we can rely on hard data – internal data. The big benefits are going to come in marketing. But marketing has to rely on managing its collection. And, to manage it, you must first establish ownership and responsibility. Marketing information comes from soft data – external data. Its collection is not an automatic by-product of some existing process. But the fact that it requires special effort has its good points. Once they accept the need for this effort, they already recognize its value.'

One of the main problems encountered when IT is decentralized is the concentration on short-term objectives. The problem arises because the construction of a corporate information system infrastructure is a complex engineering task, which, by its very nature, takes a long time and considerable resources. But investing in the future is a corpo-rate objective. Divisional objectives are usually to maximize profits this year.

Case

On his appointment, the IT director of a US manufacturing company found a major problem existed in meeting customer delivery promises. Each division had built its own IT system to solve this problem by providing detailed progress information, so that progress chasers could intervene and push urgent orders to the front. Since the products from the various divisions had common parts, success in urging one order meant delaying another. The IT director saw clearly the need for a common scheduling system. 'The trouble with that approach,' he said, 'is that it takes a long time to build the system, and it costs a lot more than the simple stop-gap systems that each of them has built on their own. And they'd suddenly find activities going on outside their control. Work patterns in the factories would be adjusted to an agreed formula for example. All strong, powerful directors want to do is to manage and control their environment – they're not too much worried by what's going on outside of it. Somehow we have to break down the barriers between directorates when we build IT systems.'

Influencing the IT policies of powerful local barons was held to be the fourth most serious problem of decentralized IT. Once again we see the organizational difficulties created when IT is in a support role, yet there is a need to impose IT strategies on the line functions in the corporate interest. The IT director has no power to insist. It all falls back onto the chief executive's shoulders.

A European food manufacturing and distribution group was in the process of decentralizing much of its IT systems in response to pressure from the directors of the various divisions. There was a clear recognition of the need for a core system however, and an IT director was appointed with the responsibility for providing it. He complained of a severe conflict of interests. 'We have this great move to make more of our systems user driven. But only 40% of our systems have specific users. The rest are infrastructures – things the whole company needs. This is how we do it. I put up a proposal to the executive committee, which is the boss and three of the group directors. Take the case where they say "Yes, it's got no users, but we've got to have it. We won't survive in five years' time without this centralized core system." This leads to huge problems down the line, because the users have to bear their share of the costs. And this affects the performance-related pay of the directors and senior managers. It creates enormous aggression. I've been to the group board five times with one case, there's so much opposition.'

Five successive stages in the way IT is organized were identified during our research. Figure 5.9 shows that decentralization started in stage two, driven by the arrival of on-line technology which made entering transactions as and where they occurred feasible, instead of batching them for delayed, centralized bulk processing.

66 The strains are evident. I'm for the first time seeking to control and coordinate people who are being paid to do their own thing 99

Case
66 We had virtually a problem of Unilateral Declarations of Independence; strong divisions, but working in isolation. Fortunately we have a brave boss. He wasn't content with the 'You just provide the money. Leave us alone and we'll come up with the goods' argument. He recognized the need to get a handle on the business, that corporate information gives the so-called competitive edge. He was determined to claw back the corporate core of our information systems. His second bravery was to appoint me as group IT director to build that core. If I fail, he fails 99

“It amounts to the boss backing me against the local barons – and on my say so. That's something he won't do lightly”

STAGE	DRIVER
I Centralization	Technical
II Centralized computer Decentralized data capture	Technical
III Decentralized business units served by IS Inc.	Business
IV Decentralized IT	Business (technical enablers)
V Core systems	Technical (business enablers)

Figure 5.9 The five stages of IT organization

Companies then embarked on strategies of decentralizing their business operations, leaving IT to be provided as a centralized service. Caught up by the mood to make everything pay its way, many IT departments were reformed as semi-independent companies, charging for their services.

Commenting on this trend, one IT director commented, 'Here, in Germany, ten years ago it was 'in' to reorganize IT as a separate company. There were ten, or fifteen, of the larger companies who had IT subsidiaries with separate managing directors. All of them failed. They lost the power to influence IT in the parent company.'

Stage four is the logical next step, and is where many companies are at present. The decentralized business units feel their muscles. And demand control over their costs and systems if they are to be held responsible for results. It is hard to resist the argument. IT gets dispersed.

“It might make sense in two or three years time. But at the present stage of enthusiastic decentralization, it's hard to see the need for the centre”

Stage five presents a difficulty if stage four has been allowed to go the whole way. Many IT directors are maintaining a passive role at present, biding their time until the company, learning from the error of its ways, welcomes some return to centralization. By that time, severe difficulties may arise however.

Case

A successful small tools manufacturer had grown its business internationally, and had production and marketing facilities in eighteen countries. It had eighteen different IT systems. The marketing director suggested it was now time to claw back some of these systems, for three reasons:

- He felt the corporate strategy should now be to assemble locally, rather than to produce locally.
- There was a need for EDI.
- Further cost reductions were possible through global rather than local sourcing.

These three strategies were each unpopular with the local companies, and they used the high costs of rewriting the decentralized IT systems as a winning argument against the proposals.

Q: What progress have you made with introducing the core system concept?

A: It's difficult. You have to show each business manager what the benefits are. He has to sub-optimize in some areas, to get benefits, longer term, in others.

Q: Isn't there going to be a problem later?

A: The reason there's ever over-decentralization is because the IT manager isn't doing his job. He lets it go because it relieves pressure. But it's no good letting the users develop the systems they think they need, and then trying to pull it all altogether at the end. We've set clear guidelines. If they do anything outside them, we want to know. You remember the days when we used to ask the users to sign their requirements specifications? We've turned that one on its head. We, in the IT department, sign off on anything that's critical to the business today.

Case

THE TOP PROBLEMS RAISED BY DECENTRALIZATION STRATEGIES ARE IDENTIFYING AND PROCESSING WHAT SHOULD REMAIN AS A CORPORATE RESOURCE.

Section 4
Life expectancy at the centre

❝ It's a permanent job. Only if you're static as a company, can you afford to be static in IT ❞

❝ The centre is a stop gap. To kick it all off. And, now the users are taking over, to manage a very difficult decentralization exercise. But IT is becoming more and more a fundamental part of every function in the business. When we achieve our goal of making every manager IT competent, and IT confident, the positioning of the centralized IT department drops from the control tower to the engine room. I give its importance five years, ten at the most ❞

❝ The need doesn't just spring from IT. Every business is going to be a series of projects, sitting on top of the factory. They will all have IT in common. There will be a need to drive them from the board. The IT director will become a projects director ❞

❝ Paradoxically, it is the very growing

A number of senior managers feel that the need for a central IT department, and for an IT director, is temporary. Two things have happened simultaneously, they argue. IT has become important, vital to the survival of the company. But the technology has appeared to enable its decentralization to the users. There is certainly a need to manage it centrally at this moment. Because IT is vital to success, corporate strategies have to be planned and implemented. There is not the knowledge or experience on the board, or in the line departments, to do these things. Hence the IT director and his department.

The department is sowing the seeds of its own destruction however. It is pushing more and more responsibility out to the users. As the users manage their own IT they acquire the knowledge and experience which was previously the monopoly of the centre. This knowledge was the only *raison d'être* of the centre. When this happens therefore, the centre will disappear.

We have discussed a number of roles however, which need to be performed centrally for reasons of coordination, rather than of knowledge. It is worth summarizing them at this point:

- Corporate activity has changed from separate functions pursuing steady objectives, to combined functions pursuing short-term and rapidly changing objectives. Project management is becoming more important than line management.
- Information is a common resource.
- Some IT and IT systems are common – the communications infrastructure and corporate database for example.
- If there are to be any responsibilities exercised at corporate level, if there is to be any corporate planning and control, there is a need for a corporate IT system.
- If there is any need to sub-optimize a decentralized system, or to incorporate standards, in the interests of the company as a whole, there is a need for central authority to insist these things are done.

An interesting debate was discovered however, on the nature of the function that should remain centralized. It turned on the issue: should we decentralize the responsibility for information sytems or the technology, the I or the T of IT? On the one hand, the view was expressed that 'We should give IT back to the business. Let the users run their own computers. All that's important is that the systems are never designed bottom up again. The role of the centre is to determine the basic information needed for corporate planning and control. And to insist that the local operational systems enable the centre to suck off the corporate strategic systems that everyone can tap into.'

Contrast this with 'At present I study the business plan, and extract the IT and the IS (Information Systems) implications. I do the IS bit, because if I didn't, no one else would. But it is the determination of information requirements that should be decentralized. Only the users know what they want to run their departments. What's wanted is that IS is given to the line, and IT is on the board. Getting the technology right is fundamental to success. This enables decentralization to take place in a healthy way, rather than through unhealthy grabbing. Building the technology infrastructure is the only centralized function.'

Both these arguments are strong pleas for co-ordination, each achieving it in different ways. There can be no doubt that there will always be a need for some centralized hardware, and some centralized systems, serving both the corporate centre, and allowing decentralized units to make use of facilities they need in common. What may be in doubt is how difficult it will be to run this centre. Whether it will merit an IT director's attention.

The summary of roles listed above suggests there will be a continuing need for central IT authority. Can this power be divorced from responsibility for business results however? We come back to this point in the final chapter.

> strength of the go-it-alone user that will ensure the continuing need for an IT supremo – to coordinate their activities, run the underlying core systems they draw on, provide the communications infrastructure they need, and design the standards so that what they do individually all hangs together **99**

> **66** We're becoming so reliant on information, that I can't believe my successor won't also be a main board director. It's finance and planning that will be redundant. With the right information systems the board can do all that for themselves **99**

98% OF IT DIRECTORS FEEL THERE WILL STILL BE A NEED FOR THEIR JOB BY 1995, AND 90% FEEL THE NEED WILL STILL BE THERE IN AD2000.

HOWEVER, THEY RATED THE RELATIVE IMPORTANCE OF THE CENTRALIZED IT DEPARTMENT TO USER-CONTROLLED IT AS FALLING FROM 75:25 IN 1995 TO ABOUT 50:50 AT THE END OF THE DECADE.

Chapter 6

Systems development

66 After 20 years, writing a lot of programs, reading a lot more, and debugging even more of them, my overall impression of our business is that we are struggling, with our unaided minds, on something far too big for us! 99

Jerry Weinberg, *The Psychology of Programming*

Section 1
Why is it such a problem?

❝ It's like your first Chinese meal. How can you say what you'd like? ❞

❝ Here's your problem. Technicians can't manage. Not other people, not even themselves. And most managers don't have a project mentality, they're trained to manage ongoing situations. Get in a good project manager, use project management principles and you meet your deadlines every time ❞

❝ How would you describe a journey into the unknown, a place where your compass doesn't work, the sun and the stars are replaced by elusive rainbows, milestones are celebrated and passed but the horizon never gets nearer. The language is strange, the customs new, the pathways intricate and mysterious and you depend on local guides and native bearers. The further you go, the more money they demand to carry on. Gradually the feeling grows that you're going where they want to take you. Does it sound at all like a nightmare? Well, it is – and one that computer managers regularly suffer ❞

In chapter 2, we described the problem of developing computer systems as one of the major constraints on further progress with IT.

At first, systems development was not recognized as a need, let alone a problem. The board assumed the computer was ready to use. They were entitled to. It was a tough proposition to grasp that anything costing that amount of money couldn't actually do anything; that as much money again, and more, and years of hard work were necessary before any useful information came out on the printer and on the screens.

Once it was appreciated that the computer was only as good as its programs, it was a natural management reaction to recruit programmers, to apply the required resources to overcome the problem. And, if the system was bigger than first realized, to apply more programmers. And if building the system was running late, to apply even more.

❝ We spent nine months talking equipment, cost/benefit analyses and systems automation. And another three sweating over signing the cheque. That done, we thought we were over the worst. No one was prepared for the millions of dollars and aeons of time to write the wretched programs ❞

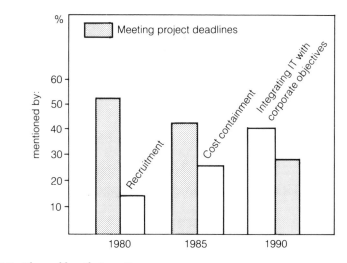

Figure 6.1   The problem that won't go away

The fact that throwing more resources at the problem didn't work came as a surprise. By 1980, the difficulty of meeting project deadlines had become the top issue for IT executives in all countries except Japan, where the systems development job was done for them by the equipment suppliers.

Figure 6.1 illustrates the main point however, that the problem was still out there in 1990, and proving as intractable as ever.

We have noted, as a key finding of our research, the fact that, when it comes to managing computers and IT in business, many of the established techniques don't seem to work.

Identifying and deploying the required resources, for example, is a normal management approach. IT directors were divided on why this method had failed. Some complained that the resources needed were just not there. 'There is a world programmer shortage,' is the cry. 'You can advertize all you like, and offer salaries way over the top – you still won't get any replies. And if you're looking for specific experience – telecommunications for example, or a particular operating system, language or application – the people are just not there in any numbers.'

Certainly the salaries paid to systems development staff in the first twenty years of the information revolution, often double that of other technicians and way outside the salary scales of a company's job grading system, supported the notion of world shortage.

But what happened to the laws of supply and demand? Admittedly, things in short supply get pricey. But high prices encourage more supplies. Until there's enough, and prices become reasonable. Well, programmers' salaries today no longer exhibit such attractive differentials from other professions. And the 1990 business recession has cut back the demand for their services. Is there still a shortage?

The argument that the job is so skilled that only a few can do it, also doesn't seem to stand up. The evidence is that one in five of any randomly selected group can write computer programs, irrespective of their education.

Case

The IT director of a large European metal products manufacturer was faced with the problem of no replies to his advertisements for systems development staff in the late '70s. He was also faced with staff retention problems, with job hopping after less than a year's service, and often before the projects they were working on went live on the computer. He advertized, inside his company, a one-day's computer appreciation course for any employees interested in a job change – and was overwhelmed by replies. Many of these were from shop floor workers and administration staff whose jobs were at risk from continued automation schemes. The one-day course described how computers worked, the job opportunities offered in IT in the company, and included a programming aptitude test. Eighteen people attended the first course. Four passed the aptitude test. They later attended an eight-week programming course and went on to successful careers as programmers. The IT director commented 'I have repeated this selection process many times since. We know now that we can rely on a twenty per cent success rate. The recruits come from all backgrounds. Some of the best left school at fifteen and are in their forties. They have some problems adapting to a new work environment, that takes time – but they have no problems with the work itself. It knocks this "we must recruit graduates" notion on the head. Also, graduates aren't content with programming. They're high flyers, and don't stay very long in the department.'

Most IT directors do not subscribe to the world shortage theory. In the short-term, there is of course a limited supply. About three million worldwide is one estimate. But in the long-term, this could easily be increased, doubled, trebled, whatever is demanded.

The truth is, these newcomers would not get jobs. There is a limit on how many new systems and systems changes an organization can take. There is a limit on how many programmers a company is prepared to employ, and attempt to integrate into its workforce.

Most important, there is a limit, and a very low one, on how many programmers can be employed on a project without getting in each other's way. Two programmers working on the same program do not halve the development time. The communications and work segregation problems involved invariably mean that the time taken is increased;

66 People always say supply tends to equal demand. They mean it equals effective demand. With my programming backlog, I have a demand for all the programmers in the world. But the company just isn't going to take on any more than we have, and it isn't going to pay them any more than they're getting. So my effective

demand is nil. It isn't hard to make supply equal demand in this case **99**

66 There is no limit to the computer systems I would like to have if I didn't have the work of developing them, or the problem of paying for them **99**

probably doubled since each will produce a different solution, and more than doubled if they are asked to sort out their differences.

If the programmer shortage is not responsible for the problem, there is an implication that, although we say we want more systems, we are not prepared to employ more resources, and therefore have come to terms with the shortfall. Why then is systems development one of the top problems facing IT directors?

The organizational split, which separates the users of the systems from the people who develop them, creates a psychological difficulty. Many IT directors claim that the constraints on employing more programmers are only experienced by the computer department, and leave the user free to demand the earth, since they do not have the responsibility of delivery.

There are two intrinsic difficulties of computer system development however, which contribute to its being one of the main worries of the IT director; they also provide further examples of the inappropriateness of established management techniques when applied in the field of IT.

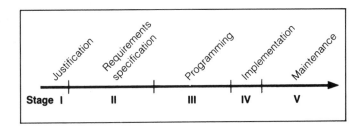

Figure 6.2   The Life Cycle approach to systems development

Case

66 No one knows what they want. But when they see what you've produced, they suddenly know what it is they don't want **99**

66 Two lines in the corporate plan equal twenty thousand lines in a system specification. We simply don't understand the business to that degree **99**

An automobile manufacturer, in the US, analyzed how programmers spent their time. They produced the following summary:

Writing	14%
Testing	38%
Delays (requirements specification queries, errors and changes	48%

This study was carried out in 1968. It led the company to identify systems analysis, and the specification of requirements, as the two key activities which governed programming productivity. Accordingly they spent many years, and a great many dollars, investigating and trying out new methods of systems analysis. Most of the methods added to the time of analyzing requirements, but without reducing the subsequent programming time. In an effort to reduce the delays, they instituted the procedure of insisting that the users signed off the requirements specification, and of then freezing the specification until the programs were written. This shortened the programming time noticeably. Before this procedure was started however, the users had complained that the systems delivered were never what they wanted, and they only acceded to them in the interests of getting something going. The frozen specification approach immediately led to an escalation of such complaints, and had to be abandoned. In 1983, fifteen years after the original study, they started to question the validity of their basic approach to systems development. This approach, known as the Life Cycle method (Figure 6.2), was the computer industry standard at the time. It was based on the assumption that each of the five stages could be completed in the sequence shown, that is that the costs and benefits of a computer system could be calculated in advance, and thus govern any decision to go ahead, that its users knew what they wanted, that the amount of programming required could be measured, and that computer programs, once written, could subsequently be altered. Each premise seemed eminently sensible, since they accorded with management findings and practice in most other fields of activity. They concluded however, that none of these premises was true in the case of computer systems development. They decided to develop a new approach to systems development based on three novel premises:

1) *The users could not be expected to know what they wanted.*
   Since the system to be developed had not been automated before, they were, in some cases, substituting untried rules for human discretion; in others, attempting an entirely new activity. No one knows, in detail, what they want, if they've seen nothing like it before. They can only suck it and see.
2) *The total programming effort required cannot be measured in advance.*
   The systems requirement was not known in detail, and the hardware and software always involved pioneering to some extent.
3) *Programs cannot be altered to accommodate any future require-ment. In fact their capacity for economic amendment is minimal.*
   The logical paths in a program of any size are so numerous and complex that it is beyond the capacity of the human brain to visualize the effect of any alteration. The solution is not to be found in better documentation. All this provides is the ability to see exactly how complex the structure is, and how foolish we would be to tamper with it.

In summary, computer systems development is difficult, not because of the shortage of competent programmers, but because it is a new and foreign activity to the business, and presents a number of problems

66 We seemed to indulge in a severe form of double-speak. With our technical hats on, we planned enthusiastically to use state-of-the-art equipment to process systems which had never been automated before. We then put on our management hats and, with perfect seriousness, wrote down how long each task would take 99

66 We have three levels of confidence in target dates. When the project is put up for a justification study and a cost/benefit analysis, I give the users an A date. This means I have no idea, and I admit it. When the system has been specified I give them a B date. This also means I have no idea, but they no longer believe me. When we have the programs designed, and coding begins, I give them a C date. I still have no idea, but a revision at this stage gives the users a lot of confidence, and generates good motivation 99

which do not succumb to traditional management techniques. These are:

- *The separation of power from responsibility.* Users have frequently had the power to demand systems without having had to bear responsibility for the systems development management problems and costs involved. This has led to an artificial level of demand.
- *The difficulty of stating what is required.* It is virtually impossible to specify needs the first time round, to the last atom of detail necessary to write computer programs.
- *The difficulty of measuring pioneering work.* Much of the work in developing computer systems breaks new ground, and the amount of work involved is therefore not known.

The Life Cycle approach, which was the industry standard for the first twenty years of computer systems development, and is still widely used today, effectively denies the existence of these three factors.

It should more properly be called the Death Cycle, since it is now clear that the hope offered by stage five, that systems built by this method could subsequently be changed and kept up to date, was spurious. Many IT directors confess that their companies are saddled with a foundation core of computer systems, laid down between 1960 and 1980, and which cannot now be altered or added to.

> IT DIRECTORS ESTIMATE THAT 35% OF THE AVERAGE
> SYSTEM DEVELOPMENT INVOLVES PIONEERING HARDWARE,
> SOFTWARE TOOLS OR THE RULES TO BE FOLLOWED BY THE
> SYSTEM.

Four main strands emerged when we investigated the solutions to systems development problems being presently tried.

1   *Contingency planning*
    Those aspects of any system development which involve pioneering are identified, isolated, tackled as research projects, promoted to the earliest point possible so that uncertainty is minimized, given proving dates, and backed by alternatives should any uncertainty remain after the proving date.

2   *Prototyping*
    The specification of requirements is evolved gradually as a result of developing and running a number of trial systems.

3   *Segmentation*
    Systems are broken down into small parts for the purpose of development and maintenance – reducing both the programming complexity, and the redundancy due to obsolescence.

4 *User responsibility*
User responsibility, rather than mere involvement, is achieved by maintaining the mixed staff project team as a permanent feature of the user department, responsible for the continued operation of the automated side of their operations.

These approaches are not new. Their adoption was inhibited, until recently, by the hardware and software available. Today's cheaper machines, improved telecommunications and faster programming languages, makes them look more promising.

It is sobering to remember however, that the problem of systems development has been one of management's chief worries ever since computers were used in business. Despite thirty years' effort to crack it, the difficulty remains one of the major constraints on IT progress.

> 41% OF IT DIRECTORS STATE THAT THEIR MAIN PROBLEM IS THE TIME TAKEN TO DEVELOP NEW SYSTEMS.
>
> 92% PUT THE PROBLEM AMONGST THEIR TOP THREE.
>
> 42% CLAIM THE REASON IS THE IMPRECISE NATURE OF THEIR CORPORATE OBJECTIVES AND THE CONSEQUENT DIFFICULTY OF SPECIFYING COMPUTER SYSTEM REQUIREMENTS.

"The technical solutions are still managed by us. But the project manager goes out and lives in user-land"

"Our computer projects started out as temporary. But they became part of the organizational structure. Take our customer service system. The project team never dispersed. We run permanent projects today"

Section 2
Systems maintenance

❝Here in Japan, maintenance used to be the number one problem. Today however, we look to replacement rather than maintenance❞

❝The time isn't far away when Wall Street will judge a company by the antiquity of its computer systems❞

❝No one discusses it – but the truth is we're crippled by our old systems. In the end a newcomer is going to take over our number one position in the industry. Think of the advantages they'll have: modular programs, open systems, Unix, programs written in C, RISC architecture – all the latest technology❞

Programs are hard to write. They are even harder to alter. Given the difficulty, we have to ask why do we try to change them?

Figure 6.3 shows that IT directors identify five main reasons for carrying out program maintenance. Every program contains mistakes. After it has been running for a year or more, one would expect most of these errors to have been identified and put right. Because it is often hard to correct errors completely, because the circumstances which expose them may not be encountered for many years, and because subsequently developed systems reveal errors which otherwise would have lain for ever undetected, the need to correct errors never completely disappears however.

Following Watershed in 1985, there has been an all-out drive to improve the efficiency of computer systems – with cost containment (getting more work through the computer, and thus avoiding buying more hardware) or even cost reduction in view. This can involve rewriting much of the original programs, which were probably put together as quickly as possible, because of the deadlines problem discussed earlier, and with little regard for how efficiently they ran on the computer.

Two other reasons for maintaining programs, but which have both declined during the last two years, are incorporating system improvements and new features requested by the users, and changing the programs so that they will run on more up-to-date equipment.

The demand for system changes to meet these needs has not declined. But management has made strong efforts to cut down on program maintenance, and resisting these pressures has been considered the lesser of two evils.

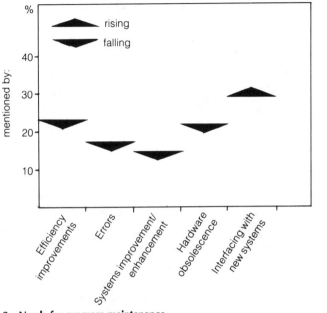

Figure 6.3   Needs for program maintenance

The need to produce entirely new systems cannot be resisted however, if the business is to stay alive. It is the unfortunate necessity to link these new systems to the old ones, and to adapt the old ones accordingly, that has given rise to a sharply growing need for maintenance.

Why does program maintenance present such a problem? One company identified four reasons:

Case

A European transport group, which had been developing its computer systems over a thirty year period, made the revolutionary proposition, in 1990, to cease all further program maintenance. They supported the proposal with the following arguments:

1) *Unjustified difficulty*
'Computer programming is impossible,' said the IT director. 'This is, unfortunately, not to say we don't try to do it. But we can't do it well. It is the sheer difficulty of the task, the intrinsic complexity of programming, that needs to be appreciated at board level. One in three instructions in a program provide the opportunity to test some condition, and go to another part of the program. Imagine all the

logical paths in a typical program of, say, 1000 instructions. It's not just 300: the number of tests. Because each test can lead you to another test. It's nearer 300 to the power 300. One of those impossible numbers! Fortunately, for the purpose of our proposal, we do not need to investigate it further. The complexity of the average program is such that it is beyond the human brain to visualize it. We can never be completely confident they will work in all circumstances therefore. And, while it is working, it is best to leave well alone. Because we can never be completely confident what effect any change we make will have. Add to this the fact that the program you are contemplating changing wasn't written by you in the first place, and you have the maintenance problem in a nutshell. If the author didn't understand it, what chance do you have?'

2) Out-of-Control

Because the company found itself in the position of not understanding their existing programs, and being unable to alter them substantially, they found themselves facing the unpalatable consequence that, as long as IT management relied on maintaining programs, they faced a potential out-of-control situation. 'The present programs were thrown together to meet deadlines, but with really no quality control,' the director commented. 'For one thing, they gave no real protection against penetration. We are currently investigating a fraud so large I can't discuss it. But it's too late to build in security routines now. Another crippling problem is that we are inhibited from bringing the company's systems up-to-date to meet the present way our competitors do business, because we daren't touch the programs – they'd fall over. The thing we dread, however, is a situation which throws the system out of action, and which we can't recover from because we can't get into the programs.'

> 26% OF IT DIRECTORS STATED THEIR MAIN CONCERN WAS THAT THEIR COMPANIES ARE AT THE MERCY OF BADLY WRITTEN AND FRAGILE PROGRAMS WHICH CAN NO LONGER BE ALTERED.

We stated in chapter 3 that one of the chief worries of a number of IT directors was that their companies could no longer function without their computer systems, but that these systems, in many cases, were no longer maintainable.

We make no excuse for repeating this statistic here. It is one of the main and most disturbing findings of our research. If its computer systems are no longer maintainable, then, by definition, a company faces a potential out-of-control situation.

❝ The prime need is to control the baroque programming we've all indulged in over the years. It's not just a cost issue, it's a system complexity issue. All the larger systems, on which our companies depend, have become, over the years, dangerously unstable. It's the result of uncontrolled minor changes. You get 'systems drift', away from the original specification, and away from the original thrust of the architecture. New loads are put on foundations laid for different purposes, and it all starts falling over **❞**

> 56% OF SYSTEMS DEVELOPMENT STAFF LEAVING THEIR JOBS GIVE 'TOO MUCH PROGRAM MAINTENANCE' AS THEIR REASON.

3)   *Motivation*

The company had experienced a high turnover of systems development staff. Although this had stabilized in the last two years, they found that the quality of staff remaining was poor and morale was low. Analysis revealed the cause was an almost universal dislike of program maintenance. 'There is no challenge in the work,' said one programmer, 'except trying to find out what the hell was in the mind of the guy who wrote the program in the first place.' The programmers also complained that what had attracted them to the work had been the opportunities for creativity that writing a new program presented. There were no such opportunities just going over what someone else had written.

4)   *Inhibition of systems development*

The fourth and seemingly overwhelming argument for removing maintenance was that the activity occupied 90% of their programmers' time. With so much of their systems development team bogged down in maintaining the old programs, they had little time to develop new ones. Those that were attempted were never completed to time, because of the continual need to redeploy the development team on keeping their old programs going. Furthermore, new systems had to be integrated with the old ones. Because proper interfaces had never been designed however, writing new systems actually created maintenance needs in the old ones.

Case (continued)

66 The old mainframe was in a 90% maintenance situation. We've retrained the staff on the new machines. Most didn't want to change, they were nervous of the new technology. What's turned them on is No Maintenance; the big switch from an all-out slog on keeping it breathing, to a 100% systems development environment 99

66 They have a higher regard for themselves – no longer as service mechanics, but as car designers 99

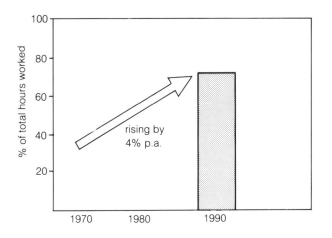

Figure 6.4   Time spent by systems development staff on maintenance

66 The maintenance problem is severe. We're just about keeping it under control with rigorous system specifications, careful documentation and tightly controlled releases 99

> 86% OF IT DIRECTORS PREDICT THAT A CONTINUED NEED TO MAINTAIN OR ADAPT THEIR OLD PROGRAMS WOULD INHIBIT ANY NEW SYSTEMS DEVELOPMENT BY THE YEAR 2000.

Figure 6.4 shows that about three quarters of the time of the world's systems analysts and programmers is now spent maintaining the programs we wrote during the first thirty years of the information revolution. It also shows that the proportion is rising steadily. Clearly a time is approaching when new development will grind to a halt. IT directors all agree something must be done about it – but not on what the solution is. There appear to be three schools of thought.

The first relies on tighter management control of the programming activity. It argues that the basic cause of the problem is that no one can understand the existing programs; not even the author. The reason is they are written in a language which instructs the computer what to do, but gives no clue as to why it is to do it.

Documentation is the answer. Flow charts and explanations, in plain English, of what each bit of the program is doing, and how it connects with the other bits.

A further cause is that continual small changes to a program confuse the user, and interfere with each other. Changes should be bundled together, rigorously tested, and then formally released in a new fully documented version.

A second school brands programming as beyond the capacity of humans to do or to manage. It recognizes that the computer itself could handle the complexity however, and pins its hopes on automation. More on this in section 5.

The third school pleads for a new approach to programming. In essence the approach is to produce throw away modules. If we can't maintain programs, we clearly can't stand still and let our existing systems restrain progress for ever! We must rewrite them. But not all of them. That's plainly impractical. Let's write them in small, separateable bits, and just rewrite the bits that need changing.

66 There are two distinct systems – the sine qua non, and the new activity 99

66 Too much cost was specific to an application 99

66 We're building

The most important approach to modularity so far to emerge is the splitting of the core of a system from its more ephemeral applications. The approach was described in section 2 of chapter 5. The core itself can also be written in separate modules however, each separately testable, performing separate functions, interfacing in carefully controlled ways, and of a handleable size and complexity. So can the applications.

Where the core system approach scores over just plain modularity is that the modules are separated according to longevity. What is expected to last, the infrastructure, goes into the core. Rewriting the core is admittedly costly and time-consuming. However, what changes each time the business plan changes goes into throw-away application modules.

The evidence seems to be that program maintenance is becoming less of a practical proposition as each year passes. It is clearly no solution to say we will not maintain our programs, unless we devise some other way to keep our computer systems in line with the company's changing needs. A minimal maintenance policy seems to offer the most promising solution.

The Classic Approach
Out of the 102 companies we studied in depth, we found 16 to be pursuing a minimal maintenance policy in some form. What follows are the four key steps taken in what might be called the classic cases.

1) *Employ a facilities management company*
   A facilities management company is given a contract to run and maintain the existing systems. The present computer, and often a number of the present staff, particularly those who prefer not to adapt to a server/workstation and analyst/programmer approach, are taken over by the management company. The contract is based on a sliding scale agreement, with the amount of processing running down over a planned timescale.
2) *Rewrite systems*
   The company, freed from its maintenance burden, rewrites its systems on a modular core/applications basis, using hardware and software based on open systems principles.
3) *Decentralize applications*
   Applications system development becomes the responsibility of the users.
4) *Adopt minimal maintenance policy*
   Maintenance of the new systems is governed by the following two rules:
   a) Of the five present causes of maintenance (see Figure 6.3 above), only errors will, in future, justify changes to a program module. Furthermore, the cases allowed will be restricted to emergencies, or to work occupying no more than 20 programmer days.
   b) In all other cases, the module involved will be rewritten.

16% OF COMPANIES NOW PURSUE A MINIMAL MAINTENANCE POLICY.

BY THE YEAR 2000 THIS FIGURE IS PREDICTED TO RISE TO 81%.

information warehouses. What we store, we want to last. It's what we do with it that changes 99

Cases

66 I was standing in one of those living museums, watching a party of school kids looking at a Victorian kitchen scene. A lady in a mob cap, and wearing an apron, was darning. 'You have to realize,' explained the teacher, 'that, when their socks got holes in them, they didn't go out and buy new ones. They mended them' 99

66 IT is fundamental to success. And we've invested the last thirty years building our IT systems. But if anyone was to ask me the way to succeed in our business over the next ten years, I'd have to say I shouldn't start from here 99

66 We behave as though we can maintain our programs for ever. But there may be no alternative to the death of a system. Nature admits it. You can't teach an old dog new tricks, she says. You'd better buy another puppy 99

Section 3
Outsourcing

❝ Contractors are used when top management lose confidence in-house ❞

❝ In the end, you have no choice. Your permanent staff see this, and they leave to get on the high salary bandwagon ❞

❝ If we're honest, we resist contractors because we resent them: the high salaries and the implication that we couldn't do it ourselves. But the truth is it makes sense. Anyone who wants to be a professional programmer, and get to the top of that profession, has to go the contractor path. He just won't get the experience hanging on to the coat tails of our old mainframe. More and more it's where the best people are going to be. And frankly, all this talk of improved program quality: does anyone seriously believe imposing standards on in-house staff is going to achieve it? But say what you want in a contract, and build in penalty clauses, and you can have all the quality you can pay for ❞

In 1985, when the world overcame its fear of the technical arguments supporting further IT spend, part of the IT budget suffering cutback was, naturally, systems development staff.

On average, the IT departments of the world shed four staff. They were never to return.

In that same fateful year, another, and related, thing happened. IT executives' intentions to employ outside contractors to develop their systems entered a new phase.

IN 1980, 6% OF THE AVERAGE SYSTEMS DEVELOPMENT BUDGET WAS SPENT ON OUTSIDE CONTRACTORS.

BY 1990 THIS PROPORTION HAD RISEN TO 32%.

9% OF IT DIRECTORS NOW OUTSOURCE ALL THEIR SYSTEMS DEVELOPMENT.

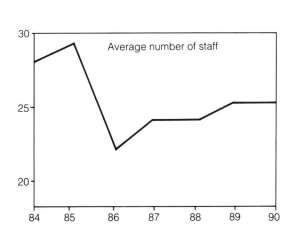

Figure 6.5   Development staff levels, 1980 – 1990

Until 1985, IT executives' intentions to use outside staff fluctuated between more and less. Since 1985 however, their vote has been for more. It has continued to fluctuate; sometimes a lot more, sometimes a little more, but always more. The result of this shift in the trend is that over a third of the world's computer systems are now developed by outside contractors. The four people in each installation who lost their jobs as a result of Watershed, were not redundant for long. Most came back to work next day as freelance programmers, and at double their old salary.

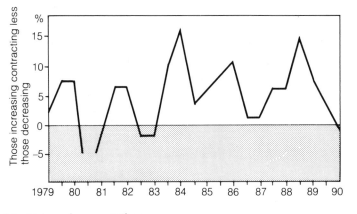

Figure 6.6   Outsourcing expectations

❝ I deplore the growth of contracting, and totally reject any suggestion that it marks the birth of a new profession. The majority of contractors are selfish, self-centered individuals who use their scant, and often over-stated experience to extort maximum rates in a shortage situation . . . etc. **❞**

Most IT directors agree that using contractors makes sense. It is a controversial area however, with feelings on the subject running high. Pride may be at stake. It is significant that IT directors (who may be reasonably expected to put business interests over professional pride) show a greater propensity to endorse policies to use contractors than do IT executives reporting at a lower level. The greatest propensity of all is displayed by IT directors with no IT background, who seem to see it as the obvious thing to do. Are they right – or is it a case of fools rush in?

Figure 6.7 displays the arguments.

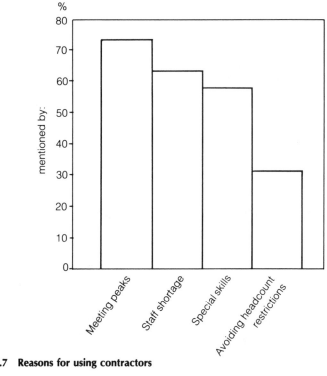

Figure 6.7 Reasons for using contractors

Avoiding headcount restrictions was the top reason in 1985, when the IT cutback began. It fell away sharply, but has shown a recent revival coincident with worldwide business recession. The main reasons however, are all to do with where the experienced staff are when they're needed. Not sitting on seats in our offices, it seems. We can't afford to keep them there – and the evidence is they don't much want to be there full-time anyway.

36% OF EXISTING IN-HOUSE PROGRAMMERS HAVE AMBITIONS TO BECOME CONTRACTORS.

58% OF EXISTING CONTRACTORS INTEND TO STAY AS CONTRACT PROGRAM- MERS ALL THEIR LIVES, EITHER AS INDIVIDUALS OR WORKING WITH A CONSULTANCY OR SOFTWARE HOUSE.

ONLY 16% OF IN-HOUSE PROGRAMMERS STATE THAT CAREER OPPORTUNITY IN THEIR COMPANY IS A REASON FOR STAYING.

As with management, the feelings of programmers on the subject also run high. There is resentment of the high earnings of contractors who sit side-by-side with in-house staff doing exactly the same job. The downside, and which holds large numbers as permanent employees, is the need to travel, and the insecurity. If these disadvantages could be overcome, there is little doubt that most IT professionals would work on their own, or for an IT consultancy or software house.

66 I wish I had the guts **99**

It makes sense. No IT professional is going to advance his skills and experience working on the same machine and applications for the rest of his career. There is a downside for IT management as well however.

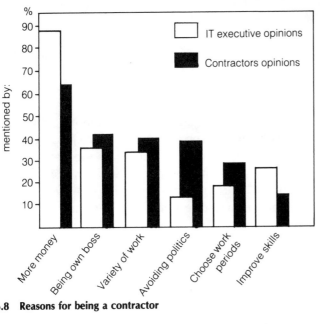

Figure 6.8   Reasons for being a contractor

The high costs of contractors were often mentioned. But protagonists were quick to point out that, on a value for money argument, contractors were often cheaper. They were consistently more productive, recruitment

66 I'm against it for all the classic reasons – high costs, you lose control, and the priceless experience of how your systems work goes out of the door 🙶

and employment costs were avoided, and you only pay for what you use. The key, and entirely valid, argument against contracting is loss of knowledge of how the company's vital systems work. This knowledge is in the contractor's head, and not in the lines of code they leave behind.

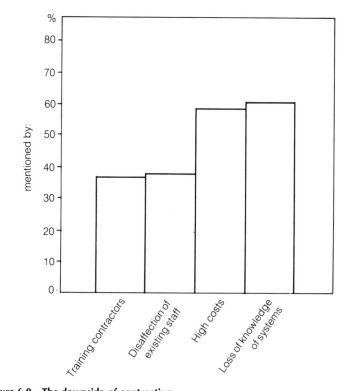

Figure 6.9   The downside of contracting

🙶 Every function in this business now depends totally on IT. To contract out our systems development is simply a dereliction of duty 🙶

There is evidence from other industries however that skills for which there is a fluctuating demand are better managed on a contract basis. Instead of discussing what proportion of our systems development we should subcontract, many IT directors felt the debate was about whether to go for the 100% option and contract the lot. If this option is chosen, the whole nature of IT responsibility and the skills required in-house undergoes a fundamental change – from activity management to contract management.

Case

The IT director of a multinational oil products company, concerned about the high levels of contracting in all its member companies, and the complaints of local IT executives, who felt the situation was getting out of control, set up a study group to investigate the problem. The study group found levels of sub-contracting varying from 15% to 40% but growing in all companies. They found that once a level of 20% contracting was reached, the nature of the IT executive's job changed, and he spent most of his time managing the contractors and dealing with agencies. They found management resented this work, as 'detracting from what they should be doing'. They found that contractors were invariably used as stop-gaps – a last resort when no permanent staff were available.

They made two recommendations:

1) *Justifying the use of contractors*
   They turned the existing policy of justifying the use of sub-contractors on its head, and recommended that it was the use of internal staff that should be justified. Contracting should be the norm. They suggested three criteria only for the use of internal staff:
   - where detailed knowledge of how the system worked was vital to survival
   - where system development demanded secrecy (for reason of fraud prevention, gaining competitive edge, etc).
   - where emergency maintenance was necessary.

2) *Reorganizing the IT department*
   They recommended that the management style and the skills retained in the IT department should be reorganized on the lines of other industries who contracted out most of their production. They cited the construction industry, which no longer employs bricklayers or plasterers for example, but concentrates on design, contract negotiation, contract management, inspection and quality control.

Is this the way systems development will go – the 100% contract option? It would tighten up professional standards. It would end the present system of two levels of remuneration for the same job – and competition would stabilize costs at a value-for-money level. It would end the fiction of pretending to provide career opportunities for professional programmers in-house. It would certainly do wonders for systems quality, since penalty clauses would ensure performance standards from the large and suable consultancy and software firms. Even individual contractors, not worth suing, would nevertheless be bound by specific performance clauses before being paid.

The weakness, inhibiting the trend at present, lies in the problem identified in section 1: the drawing-up-a-contract difficulty of specifying exactly what it is we want, and of defining program quality in anything other than weasel words like 'robust', 'secure' and 'maintainable'.

> 66 I simply don't believe programming is a proper business activity. The skills aren't related to the business, and business achievements don't motivate the programmers. They are specialists, to be brought in as required 99

> 66 We have developed a whole new technique for meeting project deadlines. We sue 99

> 66 A cultural change is needed for contract management 99

> 66 I'll tell you where the construction industry analogy falls down. We don't have any way to specify requirements like an architect can – or to see quality the way a building inspector does 99

> THE PROPORTION OF SYSTEMS DEVELOPMENT DONE
> BY CONTRACTORS IS PREDICTED TO DOUBLE FROM THE
> PRESENT ONE THIRD TO TWO THIRDS OF THE WORLD'S
> PROGRAMMING SPEND BY AD 2000.

This prediction seems to be based on the enthusiastic intentions of some IT directors, and a reluctant coming-to-terms with the situation by others.

Opinions are divided. Emotions – engendered by the high remuneration of contractors, the implied criticism when outsiders are used that 'we can't do the job ourselves', and poor-value contractors who were able to survive in the past because of the shortage situation – cloud the argument.

Those who regard contractors as a welcome addition to resources are setting about improving the way they are managed. Those who regard them as a necessary evil are deriving comfort from today's business conditions.

'Our systems development staff are no longer whiz-kid programmers,' they say. 'We now employ analyst/programmers who are more interested in business requirements than writing ingenious programs. The modern systems development aids that we have make ingenious programmers redundant. Our staff want a career with the company, they don't want to be professional programmers. Anyway, you can get all the programmers you want today. We're cashing in on the recession, and the plentiful supply conditions, to stop using contractors and build up our in-house teams.'

The next few years will show how well founded these arguments are. When the recession is over, will the contractors who have accepted in-house employment return again to their itinerant but remunerative life? Will the 37% of in-house staff, who stated their ambitions were to become contractors, put their jobs where their mouths are? Will the analyst/programmers, skilled at eliciting requirements and using simple programming tools, really be adequate to handle the demands for efficient programming when the time comes to renew or improve the company's core systems?

The dice could well be loaded. Individual contractors, and the programming agency business, may not again be the growth area that it was in the 80's. But the large firms of contractors, who accepted contractual responsibility, seem set to prosper in the longer term.

> 41% OF CONTRACT PROGRAMMERS ARE EMPLOYED BY
> CONSULTANCIES AND SOFTWARE HOUSES.
>
> THIS PRO-PORTION IS RISING BY 2% PER YEAR.

Section 4
Simplifying systems development

❝ When you look at all the programs in the world, and the relatively small number of possible applications, you wonder at all the wheels we must have re-invented. 'Ah, but our business is special!' people say. I just can't believe there's a justification for wheels of so many different shapes and sizes ❞

Two major, and successful, attempts to simplify programming have been made.

The first, which took off in a big way around 1980, was to write standard application packages. It was market-driven. There was no way all the users of microcomputers, which were then making their debut, could each justify the millions of dollars that the mainframe users had spent on making their computers work. Bespoke programming just wasn't on for the small spender.

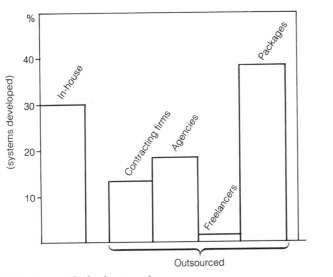

Figure 6.10   Four methods of outsourcing

Having demonstrated that a standard program could, with minor modification, satisfy the needs of many users, the idea caught on for large installations. The appeal of low cost was not the main incentive. In fact, differential pricing mechanisms meant that mainframe users paid order of magnitude increases in the price over what micro users were charged. The attraction was speed: overcoming the bottleneck of systems development caused by the time needed for bespoke programming, and the difficulty of writing tailormade programs.

> 38% OF THE WORLD'S PROGRAMS ARE NOW PURCHASED AS PACKAGES.

66 How will we all compete, when the whole world is eventually using the same package? **99**

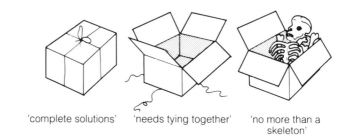

'complete solutions'   'needs tying together'   'no more than a skeleton'

Figure 6.11   The three types of package

The trend to buy packages started in the US, spread more slowly in Europe, and has only recently made much impact in Japan. After a successful honeymoon, when the benefits of packages were clearly demonstrated on standard applications like payrolls and accounting procedures, IT directors were expressing some disenchantment by the time Watershed arrived.

During our research, many mentioned the conflict between purchasing off-the-peg solutions, and using computers to get competitive edge. The following case study shows that three types of package may usefully be distinguished.

Case

An insurance company had difficulty implementing its recently defined policy of buying packages to replace its outdated 'tailormade' systems. A number of packages had been evaluated. None, however, offered scope for exploiting their new marketing strategies of 'direct quotations' and 'flexible prices', to a greater extent than those of their competitors who were installing the same packages. However, they discovered a package which provided a 'core' system, leaving them free to hang their own competitive applications onto it. Their IT director defined a new packages policy. 'Some packages provide complete solutions,' he said. 'We buy these for all applications where we seek no competitive advantage. Other packages need tying together by providing parameters. There's some scope here to beat the competition; but not much. They're mainly useful for stretching the scope of a system to suit our particular needs, but without really altering its character. A third sort of package is really no more than a skeleton. These take some implementing. No one should be fooled into thinking they're instant solutions. They take a lot of time

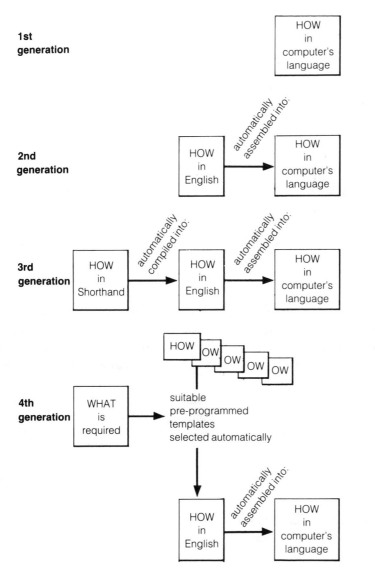

Figure 6.12   The what and the how of programming

and skill before anything's working. But they save the basic design work, and can be tailored to exploit what's unique in our products and selling strategy.'

IN 1985, 15% OF COMPUTER INSTALLATIONS EMPLOYED 4GLS.

BY 1990, THERE WERE NO INSTALLATIONS NOT MAKING SOME USE OF THEM.

❝ The productivity gains claimed for 4GLs have to be interpreted carefully. On something completely standard, like a spreadsheet for example, the gain is twenty to even a hundred-fold in some cases. On specific applications we achieve between two and threefold productivity improvement. And on some specific applications, where computer processing efficiency is vital, we can't use them at all ❞

The second successful attempt to simplify programming began to gain favour around 1985. It was the use of the so-called Fourth Generation Language (4GL). The first generation spoke directly to the computer. Very soon a second generation appeared which used plain language.

By the early sixties a third generation of languages was being used which enabled programmers to write programs more quickly, using a sort of shorthand, which is then compiled automatically into the computer's own language.

The fourth generation employs a different principle. These languages actually drive packages, or program templates, which have been prewritten, and have solved the basic strategy problems before programming starts.

It's really the difference between WHAT and HOW.

First, second and third generation languages specify HOW the computer is to do a job. This takes a lot of skill and a lot of time. 4GLs only specify WHAT the computer is to achieve, how it does it is already sorted out in the template. This difference explains both the advantage and the disadvantage of the 4GL. If there is a suitable template for your application, it enables very fast programming. And it deskills the job to a great extent. If there isn't you can't use a pure 4GL. You have to use a sort of cross between a 4GL and a 3GL. This is slower to use, and needs programming skills.

Both 4GLs and the hybrids can, at times, make inefficient use of computers, since they employ standard strategies, and cannot make use of the programmer's ingenuity to optimize the way they work.

There have been many attempts to solve the systems development problem: technical, organizational, methodological and managerial panaceas have been offered. They have come and they have gone. We have described packages and 4GLs as successful however. But they have not proved to be panaceas. It is important to define this success therefore.

Our research showed that IT directors felt that packages had solved the problem of programming standard applications. Solutions could be bought off the shelf. This accounts for some 30% of their programs. But, by definition, they account for none of their systems development work. This has grown, in accordance with Parkinson's law, to fill the world's programming capacity.

Tailoring packages, and using 4GLs, is a lot easier than writing in a 3GL, or a 2GL, however. The main effect of this has been to allow users to do their own programming, and to improve the productivity of professional programmers. But, once again, Mr Parkinson has stepped in, and demand still exceeds supply.

BY 1995 IT IS PREDICTED 75% OF SYSTEMS DEVELOPMENT
WILL BE CARRIED OUT BY THE USERS THEMSELVES, OR
BY PROGRAMMERS UNDER THEIR CONTROL, AND USING
TAILORABLE PACKAGES AND 4GLS.

NO IT DIRECTOR INTERVIEWED, HOWEVER, CLAIMED THAT
THE USE OF PACKAGES OR OF PURE 4GLS WOULD ACCOUNT
FOR MORE THAN 30% OF HIS PROGRAMMING EFFORT,
OR THAT THEY WOULD SOLVE THE CENTRALIZED SYSTEMS
DEVELOPMENT PROBLEM.

Section 5
Automating systems development

❝ Why can't the computer write its own programs? ❞

❝ Computer experts have automated every one else's work. It's time they took a dose of their own medicine ❞

❝ When we have the tools and disciplines to build comprehensive models of the thing we're engineering, only then can we call ourselves engineers. And only then will the computer be able to help us in our work ❞

❝ There are impressive claims for improved productivity. But if we were forced to put in a system in a few days, do we believe we could? ❞

❝ To recruit a graduate today, you have to put enough IT on their desks to launch a satellite ❞

❝ What has CASE done for us? It's pleased the systems developers. They can play around with computer screens now, just like other engineers. It's forced us to spend a lot more time specifying requirements. We don't understand them any better, but we spend a lot more time trying. It's totally baffled the users. This has

Programming is complicated. But the process is logical; it follows rules. Given an objective, the construction of a system to achieve it can be optimized. The fact that this can only done with hindsight, and then never perfectly, is because the task involves the consideration of too many alternatives for the human brain to manipulate. But this juggling and optimization of alternatives was just what computers were invented for.

The thought that the computer could do its own programming, and thus take the systems development problem out of its permanent ready-next-week state, and turn it into a manageable task, is irresistible. However, progress in realizing this thought has been patchy.

The two main possibilities offering scope for automation are found in analyzing and specifying system requirements, and in writing, testing and maintaining programs. The tools for realizing these possibilities, some of which, like sort generators and report generators, are nearly as old as computers themselves, have now been collected together, under the generic name of CASE tools. CASE stands for computer aided software engineering. It is divided into upper case, which embraces the requirements specification activity, and lower case, devoted to automating programming.

The automation of programming includes that of maintaining programs, and the particularly important possibility of moving programs written for one machine, and in one language, to others; and of improving their efficiency and structure in the process. This process of automatically improving existing programs is known as reverse engineering. When an entirely satisfactory set of CASE tools appears, reverse engineering will be vital if we are to apply them to the enormous world investment residing in its existing programs.

But the problem does not seem to lie in the lower case area. Programs can be generated automatically from tight specifications of requirements. The difficulty is that there are, as yet, no generally accepted methods for producing sufficiently tight specifications.

A large professional institute, embarking on improving its computer-based membership records and subscriptions system, made use of CASE software to analyze its requirements and produce a specification.

The software enabled them to record the different items of information used by their organization, and explore the relationships each item had with all the others. A team of five analysts worked for three months on the project, but failed to produce an agreed specification, and work was suspended. 'Upper CASE relies on data relationship tools to model requirements,' commented the IT director. 'After modelling our organization's data in this way, we found that data doesn't have inherent relationships. Relationships are arbitrarily assigned to

restored the self-respect of the professionals, who've taken a bit of a battering from all the deskilling of the last few years. And it's cost us a fortune **99**

Case

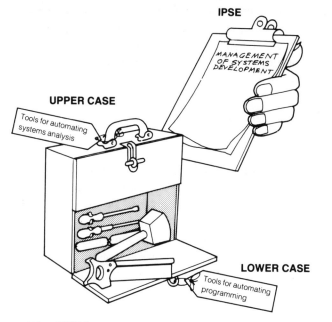

Figure 6.13 What CASE does

suit the purpose for which the data is used. This gave us two major problems. Firstly, there is no end to the number of relationships that can be explored. Each of our analysts produced their own, different model, and would have gone on refining it for ever if I hadn't called a halt. Unless somebody introduces agreed objectives into the study, you can do an awful lot of work and get nowhere. Secondly, without objectives, the only requirement you can model is that of holding a database. Now our organization isn't here to construct and maintain a database – and I don't think anybody else's organization is either. We're here to make use of it. But CASE never asked us about that!'

> 45% OF IT DIRECTORS PRAISED THE ACHIEVEMENTS OF CASE.
>
> ONLY 8%, HOWEVER, CLAIMED WORTHWHILE IMPROVE-MENTS IN THEIR OWN SYSTEMS DEVELOPMENT.
>
> MORE THAN ONE IN FIVE OF THOSE PIONEERING THE USE OF CASE TOOLS HAVE REJECTED THEM.

❝ It forces us to understand our business, because it forces us to describe its requirements as an engineer, not just by saying 'there's a customer out there somewhere! ❞

The support of CASE shown by IT directors contradicted the lack of achievement demonstrated by the use of the tools presently available. It appeared to be based on a clear appreciation of their potential, and on some wishful thinking concerning the current state of the art.

Statements emphasizing the attention CASE forced systems developers to pay to analysis, even to the extent of slowing up systems development, but with a payoff later, since carefully engineered systems did not need so much maintenance subsequently, were remarkable – if only for the fact that no one has yet been using full-blown CASE tools long enough to know what the long-term maintenance situation will be.

For all its present shortcomings, there can be no doubt that CASE could eventually provide the long-term answer to the systems development bottleneck.

❝ CASE equips you with the tools to build an engineering model of the business. It provides the greatest opportunity to deskill code cutting, and have systems developers concentrate on business requirements ❞

Constructing computer systems is a form of engineering. Engineering requires models to be built, using precise drawing or descriptive tools. Design and construction problems are exposed and resolved by reworking the model. The real thing is then built. The computer has helped engineers in general by enabling them to achieve order-of-magnitude time and accuracy improvements in building models. It has then been able to automate much, and often all, of the final construction.

Systems engineering will, eventually, prove to be no different from the other engineering disciplines in benefiting from CAD/CAM – to the point of being transformed by it. But we may have to wait a long time.

Information systems engineers practice a young science. We have to recognize that the tools the other engineering professions use for modelling were developed over centuries; mathematics for actuaries, physics for mechanical engineers, mapping for surveyors and scale drawing for architects for example.

We like to think we have these tools in the IT profession. Management see the need to engineer their company's information systems, software suppliers want to market CASE tool packages, the systems developers want to be thought of as engineers and construct their systems on computer screens.

But the truth is we cannot yet build models of information systems which can represent all our requirements, and enable us to play with them until we are satisfied they are structurally sound and cover everything the user wants. It is not the computer software that is lacking. We have not yet evolved a satisfactory information systems modelling technique for the software to drive.

> 81% OF IT DIRECTORS BELIEVE THE ONLY HOPE FOR RESOLVING THE PROBLEMS OF SYSTEMS DEVELOPMENT AND MAINTENANCE LIES IN THE POSSIBILITY OF AUTOMATING THE TASK.
>
> 66% EXPECT THIS TO BE ACHIEVED BY THE YEAR 2000.

Chapter 7

Measuring benefits

❝I come from a school which says 'If you can't measure it, you can't improve it. Because you don't know if it's got bigger or not!❞

❝It's like there was a spontaneous conspiracy to exaggerate the benefits❞

❝IT is a much more fundamental enabler than people realize. One of its first major manifestations was the printed word. But we don't cost/justify our investment in learning to read and write❞

❝Value for money needs a redefinition. I said to the business restructuring group, 'If I took your IT out on Friday night, how much money could you bring in on Monday morning?' The answer was 'Nothing.' They couldn't earn a penny. IT had become a fundamental part of their operation❞

Section 1
What are the benefits of IT?

❝ The IT budget nowadays would be 25% of the total spend. We're providing technology to the salesmen and the dealers. We're making it easy for them to do their job. They think they can't manage without it. But you tell them what it costs – and they can! ❞

❝ The main benefit of all the IT systems we've put in is that we couldn't afford the people now ❞

This chapter perpetrates a heresy. Lord Acton* would not have liked it. His disciples will no doubt seethe in anger. But it is a clear finding of this research that there is, as yet, no accurate way of measuring the benefits of IT.

> 83% OF IT DIRECTORS ADMIT THAT THE COST/BENEFIT ANALYSES SUPPORTING PROPOSALS TO INVEST IN IT ARE A FICTION.

If we cannot measure a thing, the argument goes, it is doubtful if it exists. This thought has crossed the minds of many of the world's chief executives.

Case

The chief executive of a large multinational company, concerned over the level of expenditure on IT, stated the main problem was that senior executives were sceptical about the benefits achieved. There was no clear way these benefits could be measured. This meant IT investment proposals could not be properly assessed, and the subsequent achievement could not be demonstrated.
He called for a study of the problem. Part of the study team's report follows:

'We list below eight causes of the difficulty:

* Readers will be familiar with Lord Acton's famous claim: 'Everything that exists, exists in a quantity and can therefore be measures.

1) *Backshop applications*
The early application of computers was in the backshop, to automate the administration procedures. The only direct benefits of this are administration cost savings, that is, doing what we were already doing cheaper. Administrating better, or in a new way, can never be justified by measurable benefits – since the backshop is only there to enable the frontshop, the production and selling functions, to perform. By performing better or worse, the frontshop makes profits or incurs losses. But the backshop is simply the overhead cost of having a frontshop.

2) *Frontshop applications*
Computers are becoming used, more and more, in the frontshop, on production and marketing applications to improve market share. There is no accurate measure of how much market share we will capture however. It is a guess. The justification of IT spend in the frontshop involves assessing and taking business risks.

3) *Up-front costs*
Over 60% of our computer costs are involved in developing, and running, systems which have no specific use. These systems provide the infrastructure which enables subsequent computer applications to be implemented. Since they have no specific use, they have no specific benefit. Furthermore, many of the subsequent applications which they enable are only identified five or ten years after the infrastructure investment takes place.

4) *Large lumps*
Incremental investment in IT has to be incurred in large lumps, instead of in small bits at a time. To do X, we frequently have to buy more hardware than X requires, and have to search for other uses to justify the investment. The benefits from these other uses are sometimes described as artificial, contrived or scraping the barrel.

5) *Indirect benefits*
The purpose of an organization is to satisfy its customers' needs. The computer is rarely a direct contributor to corporate purpose, however. Its users satisfy customer needs. The computer's purpose is to help the users perform this task (see Figure 7.1). Investments which are one stage removed from the company's purpose in this way are harder to justify, since the payoff does not depend on how well the investment is conceived and managed, but on how well others perform.

6) *Centralization*
Because of the high cost, the lumpy nature of the investment, and the

> " The benefits don't arise where the costs lie "

> " It's not like the old days, when we used to take out a few clerks. Now that we're using IT to capture or defend market share, how can you say what the benefits will be – to the point of justifying how much you should be spending? "

> " The well-intentioned assertion that you can do cost/benefit analyses of each system, and decide whether to go ahead, does us a disservice. Because, finally, they're all integrated. You have to take a holistic view. What is the totality of 25 systems worth to us? "

> " There is no value in information per se. Only in the use you make of it "

fact that its use is shared by many departments, computers have usually been run as a centralized 'management services' operation. This has divorced the people who can get the benefits from those who plan the IT investment. This, in turn, gives rise to difficulties in estimating and committing to benefits at the justification stage, and in achieving them in practice.

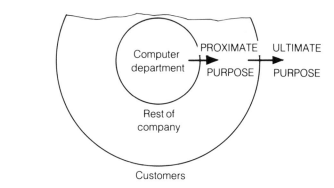

Figure 7.1   Ultimate and proximate purpose

7) *Intangible benefits*

The deliverables, resulting from computer investments, are control systems, or information systems, or both. The benefits from improved control and better information are generally not 'hard', in the sense that they can be seen, like a product improvement can. This has given rise to a class of benefits known as 'Intangibles', where the approach to measurement has been to assume an arbitrary revenue improvement, or cost reduction, in the areas making use of these systems. Unfortunately, the bulk of IT justifications usually depends on these arbitrary assessments of intangible benefits.

8) *Independent justification*

The main benefits of using computers comes, not from automating what we are already doing, but from doing something new. This new thing never results simply from implementing a computer-based system. Associated changes and investments have to take place in other areas of the company; in production, marketing, organization and corporate strategy, to get any benefit. Attempts to justify IT investment in isolation, in its own right, so to speak – a practice which is prevalent in our organization – are unrealistic.

9) *IT understanding of the cheque signers*

The size of the IT investment means that the cheques are usually signed at board level. There is a lack of understanding amongst the board, however, about the nature of the investment they are making.

> **❝** Justifying IT investment is like doing a full cost/benefit analysis on the wings of an aircraft. It isn't the wings on their own that make it fly. But it sure as hell can't fly without them! **❞**

> **❝** I have tremendous sympathy for my boss. He has to go along with what I say in

It is a formidable list. The computer seems to have hit all the awkward compromises that accountants have had to make to justify indirect costs and overheads, and then some! The clear implication of points 1 and 2 of the case study – that backshop improvements are not directly related to the bottom line, and frontshop improvements involve business risk and are equally unmeasurable – is that the only measurable and directly attributable benefits of applying IT are cost savings.

Or, to turn the coin over, all the problems of justifying IT disappear if you can make savings. It is small wonder therefore, that the hidden agendas, so frequently reported in this book, are widespread. While we insist on justifying IT investments by showing measured benefits, we restrict their use to doing what we are doing at the moment, but cheaper.

The days, however, when we could make savings by investing in IT, are largely over. Some argue they never existed. If we make administration savings today, it is by replacing out-of-date computers with cheaper IT alternatives. Which, of course, still begs the question of why we made the investment in the first place. The politically expedient way, and, if measured benefits are insisted on, the only possible way to make intelligent investments in IT, is to justify them by cost saving applications. These are benefits which will either not be achieved, or which are no more than a palliative masking the real purpose of the IT investment, which is to change the way business is done.

What is irritating about this finding of our research is that most investment in business today falls into one or more of the categories identified in the case study. The larger, and the more complex, organizations become, the less they spend on materials and on direct production and selling resources. The spend shifts into building marketing, production and administration platforms which enable cost performance improvements in the front shop. In essence, we spend more on indirect costs, to achieve reductions in the directs. It follows that investment is more and more justified by indirect rather than direct benefits – more and more by business judgement rather than black-and-white cost/benefit analyses. What is so different about IT that makes the board less comfortable with the investment proposals in this area than investing in a new factory for example?

There seem to be four differences which account for the difficulty boards have in justifying IT spend.

1 IT demands change

The application of IT involves providing a new control system, or a new information system. There is no point in changing the existing systems however, unless the behaviour systems also change. To

66 most cases, or call in outsiders to audit it. To see someone spend two billion dollars a year, and know you can't check him is an unhappy situation 99

66 Savings used to mean taking out clerks. But we've done all that. Savings today means taking out old computers 99

66 Why aren't R and D, and advertising, under the same pressure to show value for money? 99

66 Most of our top executives would say we haven't been getting the benefits. They're right. Because we fail in implementation. There's no change in the way the users do things. We automate their quill pens, but they go on using them 99

> Although I'm more aware of the value of information than any other member of the board, I'm also aware of the pitfalls of accepting responsibility for it

> Any system which centralizes local knowledge, or a previously decentralized decision, attacks a manager's authority and prestige. Any system which incurs costs for the good of the company rather than the good of a department, attacks a manager's pay

> Strategic decisions cannot be supported by operational arguments. For example, the autobahns cannot be justified by the number of cars using them. They were built to provide the flexible deployment of wartime resources

> To maintain market share, he believed he had to open seventeen more offices. Now this decision is just as hard to measure as any IT project. Yet somehow we allowed him to defend his business judgement in that area. What it amounts to is that we go paranoid if anyone goes into the boardroom with a proposal that has a technology label on it

get the benefits of IT, people have to change the way they do things, the way they manage, even the way they think. And the effects are ubiquitous and felt, not just in the department deploying IT, but amongst its suppliers, customers and other departments in communication with it. This need for fundamental and ubiquitous behavioural change is rare with other forms of investment.

2   Responsibility for achieving benefits is unclear
Where investments are made in one department, and the benefits arise in another, responsibility for getting the benefits is often unclear. Where it is left to the IT department to achieve them, they rarely have the power to do so. Where the users are nominated, they often lack the motivation to do so. In the case of core systems (the bulk of IT investment today) the users are frequently not identifiable when the investment is made.

3   Resistance from autonomous factions
Information systems and control systems strike at the root of a manager's job – and thus of his prestige and his power. Automation thus not only demands change of a manager, it can also deprive him of the exclusive use of information, and take away his authority or ability to control certain operations and to take certain decisions. On top of this, there are numerous cases where the costs of unwelcome systems have had to be borne by the managers who, overtly or privately, opposed them, sometimes suffering a loss in performance-related pay. Benefits are sometimes not reaped therefore, since the systems are subverted, and lead to unjustified pressure for decentralization.

The above three findings are significant, and go some way towards explaining the concern directed at IT investment, and which other equally judgmental investments escape. The one explanation which is unique to IT however, and is sufficient to account for all our difficulties on its own, is the fourth finding outlined below:

4   Unchampioned strategies
The days when we thought IT was to make operating improvements are gone. IT involves new business strategies. Strategies, by definition, cannot be supported by operational improvements. They involve business risk, and must be supported by the judgement, and what is vital, the commitment to make them work, of those who propose them. IT investments are frequently made without a clear understanding at board level of the new strategy involved, or of conviction at that level that the strategy will work, and without a champion at that level with the responsibility to see that it does.

THE INTANGIBLE NATURE OF COMPUTER BENEFITS IS
AMONGST THE TOP FIVE PROBLEMS FACING IT DIRECTORS,
AND HELD TO BE THE MAIN PROBLEM BY 27%.

Section 2
Soothing paradigms

❝ We get proposals supported by a business case prepared by the users. They put their anatomy on the line. We can nail every item ❞

Since IT presents such difficult investment problems, it was perhaps to be expected that our research should discover a number of popular myths, preserved more for the comfort they afford the decision maker than for any factual support. It is not so much that they are false. As with all myths, there is often a strong element of truth. But, followed in their entirety, they not only mislead, they mask the basic nature of the problem: that the board is not yet able to take business risk in the area of IT with the confidence that they display in other areas.

Paradigm 1 *IT is a support and not a line function*
There are two sorts of activities; those that earn the bread, and those that sustain and facilitate the breadwinners. It follows that the costs of breadwinning activities are 'important', and can be justified by measured returns – whereas support activity costs are a burden on the breadwinners. Support is hard to justify in accountancy terms. It is nice to have when times are good. But it is rarely necessary, and much can be dispensed with when times are bad. It also follows that the directors and managers of breadwinning activities, the makers and sellers, are important chaps, and are responsible for achieving the company's objectives. Those in support activities live vicariously, however. They cannot achieve business results, they can only help others to achieve them.

Soothing effect This gets the IT department off the hook, since, as a support function, it can never be responsible for identifying or getting benefits. It also soothes the users who feel justified in criticising the computer as an addition to the overheads.

This paradigm was never completely true. It was more true when business, agriculture, warfare were unsophisticated tasks, carried out by relatively self-sufficient individuals. The Ancient Briton had little need of

❝ We can tie the benefit down. But it's a tiered thing. Production and marketing are the only functions at the sharp end, and who thus have a direct effect on revenue. So you have to ripple it through: say What difference does this IT investment make to performance at the sharp end? It has to be one of these three things: reduce their costs, increase their revenue, or protect it ❞

❝ The only way companies will compete in future is through better software ❞

support in battle. He probably prepared his own woad, sharpened his own flints and leapt, unbriefed, into the fray. His victorious Roman adversary however, was greatly dependent, not only on his armourer, but on academia for his strategic theory and training. Today's frontline soldier is totally dependent – on the design and supply of weapons, and on electronic control systems. Tomorrow's frontline soldier will not exist. If wars are fought at all, they will be fought entirely by the so-called support functions in the back room. Frontliners will fulfil support roles, coming in afterwards to mop up, show the flag and sign the peace treaty.

Conclusion   If IT is a support function, then it provides vital, not optional support. It is a form of support which determines the way the line functions operate. It may so fundamentally determine these operations that it becomes a line function in its own right. It is certainly a determining, rather than a support factor in most strategic investment decisions.

Paradigm 2   *Investment decisions are based on cost/benefit analyses* Decisions concerning the major investments undertaken by all organizations are based on accountancy statements showing whether the financial return on the money invested satisfies the investment expectations. It follows that management's objective is to minimize investment risk, ideally to remove it altogether, by making use of calculations which add up all the costs involved, add up all the benefits and, subtracting the former from the latter, indicate mathematically the proper course of action.

Soothing effect   This paradigm encourages a board, unversed in computers and unaware of the change they wreak on the business, to approve IT investment proposals where the benefits exceed the costs. These benefits may be given a monetary value by whatever means, and despite the fact that they are not really known or committed to in many cases.

This paradigm has never fitted the facts. It may be true for shareholders, accountants and business analysts, who have no personal interest in, or responsibility for, the organization's activities. But for the managers, decisions are largely based on personal conviction. This conviction will form out of intuition, a sense of opportunity, the urge for power and plaudit, the urge to create and improve, political expediency and persuasive rhetoric. For proof, the reader has to look no further than into his own heart. It is the word 'based' that is the key. Decisions are based on human motivational factors. Accountancy statements are produced subsequently. Their purpose is valuable, as a check on affordability, deception, cashflow and foolish impracticability.

❝ For today's 'just in time' production methods, only the computer can set the stopwatch. Product quality is governed by the use of information technology. Almost every process benefits from computer aided design and manufacturing. Decision making increasingly relies on manipulating computer-based models. More and more, effective selling means capturing suppliers, agents and customers in an information net, on which they come to depend. The very goods themselves are becoming so intimately connected to conditions, instructions and guarantees, that it is becoming hard to tell whether customers buy the product, or the information layer which surrounds it **❞**

❝ Our IT costs exceed our raw materials. And all the value in our products is IT. Customer choice is based on our IT system. The product results from the optimization of production choices, based entirely on an IT model **❞**

❝ Let's not kid ourselves that investments are made in ways that are taught in the business schools – in rational ways. Management is irrational. It forms a view of the world, and makes judgments. Why should IT investment be different from any other investment **99**

Case

66 Cost savings are the only terms acceptable. We implement a vision, shared only by a few therefore. For the rest, the goals are disguised as a series of cost saving steps **99**

66 Being perfectly cynical, there's no way we'd have achieved our new core systems approach, but for the growing awareness of the unacceptable cost of the old systems. Saving money gave me the muscle to build the systems the company really needs **99**

66 Why do users go ahead when there's no obvious benefit? Because there's no obvious cost! **99**

They can form a basis for detailed planning, and for subsequent audit. They are also used to convince others; when the figures may sometimes be massaged one way and another, to support various points of view.

In a case, too well-known to give much detail or anonymity would no longer be preserved, a company dramatically increased its turnover through the use of computer terminals placed on their sales agents' desks. But the board's perception right through the implementation of the system, and for some time afterwards, was that brochures sold their products. The IT director had a conviction that availability details, displayed and interrogated on a screen at the point of sale, would increase sales. He persuaded the board to go ahead on the basis of cost savings however.'

Conclusion The implication for IT investment justification is very strong. If there is no IT champion on the board, then IT protagonists, who, like all protagonists, would normally carry the day, or lose it, on persuasion based on personal conviction, are forced to rely on accountancy statements because they are not members of the decision making team. The normal decision making process is short-circuited therefore. In its absence, the accountancy statement has to fulfil a crucial role for which it is neither intended nor suitable. This paradigm encourages hidden agendas.

Paradigm 3 *The value of IT is the price users are prepared to pay for it* If the total computer costs are analyzed by application, and then charged to the users, preferably on a pro rata basis according to use they make of the machine, then the value for money problem disappears. It disappears for three reasons:

- It is the users, not the IT department, that know the value of a computer application, and have the power and motivation to achieve it.
- The fact that they pay for an IT service means that they consider it worth the cost.
- The computer no longer costs anything, since all its costs are recovered. Indeed, if a charging system is introduced, the IT department may be reconstituted as a service bureau, sometimes as a separate company, and, if the charge rate is suitably adjusted, may actually make a profit.

Soothing effect Charging for computer services is good for the board, since it eases the IT justification dilemma, and it is good for the IT department, who feel they are no longer a cost centre but a profit centre, or, at least, a break-even centre.

This paradigm is so clearly false, it is surprising it is ever argued. One of the main reasons IT investment is difficult to justify is that so much of the cost is common to many applications, and can only be apportioned on an arbitrary basis. It is also highly disputable whether what the users are forced to pay represents their vote on value received. What else can they do but pay up? Going to an outside service bureau is not a practical proposition in most cases; it would involve a fundamental policy change.

Conclusion Undoubtedly such systems make the user more cost conscious. Undoubtedly they tighten standards and quality in the IT department, who are now on their mettle to satisfy paying customers. In practice, a transfer charging system can have quite the reverse effect from the one intended, however. The users resent paying for systems largely yielding corporate and strategic benefits, rather than operating benefits in their department, and over which they have no control. It can lead to criticism and some estrangement of the IT department, and, at worst, to unjustified pressure for decentralization and departmental go-it-alone IT policies.

The above are the major myths. A number of minor ones are worth mentioning, however:

- *Computers replace people*
  Computers are rule-following machines. Unless we can find a human being who is behaving entirely as a robot, we cannot replace them with a computer. By taking over the rule-following task, computers release rather than replace people. The benefit comes from what they get up to when they have been released.

- *IT spend should be a given proportion of the corporate spend*
  There are no prizes for winning or losing an IT spending race.

Soon after I was appointed IT director, I went to one of these Value for Money seminars. There were 42 people there. I sat still for an hour. I couldn't believe what they were saying. Basically it was 'If the business turnover is 500 million, we ought to be spending 5 million on IT. Or 50 million. Some rule of thumb.' They argued a lot over the right percentage. To me, all my life a businessman, it just didn't gel. I could

> 66 Charging the user fobs off the problem of value for IT money onto the operating areas of the company, instead of resting it on the heads of the strategy planners where it belongs.
> Our main problem is the integration of IT with the rest of the company. But charging the users for costs they can't control is actually divisive 99

> 66 We've gone away from transfer charging to responsibility for minimizing costs 99

Case

> 66 About four years ago we took the view we were low spenders

in IT. We didn't want to be high – but certainly not low **99**

66 In my view, CSFs are the bridge in integrating IT strategy and corporate strategy. Is this application important for the business, or not? **99**

feel no relationship to that. I couldn't contain myself. In the end, I got up. I said 'I'm here to learn how to get value for money, and what you're telling me is that I should spend, spend, spend. I can't accept it.' They looked at me as though I was an alien!'

- *Aiming computer applications at a company's Critical Success Factors ensures value for money.*
  Taking a reasonable percentage of the sums involved, or at stake, will enable a cash figure to be put on the potential benefits. It doesn't ensure value, nor is there any rationale equating these 'potential' benefits with what can really be expected. It is a reasonable start point. But there are too many examples of the technique being used to justify an IT investment which has already been decided on.

- *There is no such thing as an 'intangible' benefit.*
  The only benefits that count at the end of the day are monetary, that is, that add to profit. A milder version, often heard in government and non-profit making organizations, is 'the only benefits that count at the end of the day are measurable. That is to say, if you can't measure it, it doesn't exist. There are innumerable examples of generally approved human behaviour, which have no chance of providing a measurable return, using monetary units or any others. For example, having children, or installing telephone systems. With hindsight, we can put figures on some change, but the changes we measure are seldom solely attributable to the child or the telephone.

- *Expressing income as a return on investment gets over the arbitrary write-off period involved in allowing for depreciation.*
  No it doesn't. They are the same thing. It just sounds better.

Section 3
Realistic solutions

❝ There's no way a mathematical cost/benefit analysis is worth the paper it's written on ❞

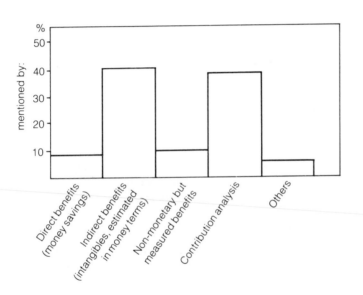

Figure 7.2 IT justification methods

It seems hardly anyone believes in cost/benefit justifications of IT investments. Only 17% of IT directors consider it a valid technique to cost/justify IT investments in isolation. Figure 7.2 shows how loathe we are to dispense with the technique however. Nearly a half of the IT spend is justified on its own, instead of as part of a corporate plan, and justified using methods which attempt to measure the benefits in monetary terms.

During our research, four alternatives were discussed.

1 *A new model*

There is great reluctance to give up on measurement. 'I don't like this judgmental or intuitive 'based on experience' approach,' said one IT director, echoing the remarks of many. 'We ought to be able to build a model to value control and information availability. If we treated these resources like a factory, or like labour. But we don't. We don't treat accountants that way, for example. What is the value to a company of

❝ Using mathematical models, with exponential formulae – it's ridiculous to consider them as appropriate. How do you account, within such a model, for the changing knowledge of the organization? It's like using a return on investment argument for educating your children. We're trying to formulate some assessment exercise for IT which says the same thing the balance sheets say, and it doesn't work! ❞

Case

50 accountants? They provide the information necessary to tell you what is happening. But we can't model the effect. Information is becoming the primary resource. We need some new, respectable models which recognise this. There aren't any good ones; not yet!'

Alternative models were discussed, and which purported to value information. But no IT director we interviewed was actually using one to justify IT investment.

2   Competitive edge

This approach has, as its key component, the identification of a use of IT which will enable the business concerned to capture market share. The benefit is estimated at the justification stage as the profit on the extra sales anticipated. It is an IT-led strategy, but is really no more than a special case of the business risk approach described below. We single it out because of the attention paid to it at the end of the '80s.

Three difficulties with the approach were identified. Firstly, many IT directors said that, although they were convinced competitive edge would be achieved, and events showed they were right, the board had not been prepared to back the project as a business risk, and the scheme had had to be sold on the basis of clerical savings.

A European public utility claimed three important benefits resulting from its customer services system. 'When customers came in, the service engineers used to rummage through filing cabinets, now it's all there on the screen. There's enormous productivity gains here. And out on the district as well, because when the vans radio in for their next job, the system gives them optimized calls, depending on priorities, where they are and so on. The biggest benefit is to customers who now get intelligent answers over the phone, because the receptionist has got the screen there in front of her. But we couldn't put a figure on these benefits when we put up the scheme. We still can't, even though it's been voted a success for three years now. So we tried to justify it on direct manpower savings.

The second objection was that such competitive advantage was shortlived, and companies should recognise the real benefit was to be a leader in a new way of doing business, which all their competitors would soon adopt.

It was also pointed out that, whilst many examples of competitive edge through the use of IT could now be found, very little of the total IT spend was devoted specifically to these applications, and they did not contribute much to the justification of the total IT budget.

3   Business risk

This approach recognizes that IT investment is no different from the majority of other investments. There is no clearly identifiable benefit that we can measure and be sure we will achieve. There are four key factors to the approach.

Firstly, the IT application is part of an overall plan, involving action and resources from other departments to achieve the objective.

Secondly, it is a belief that is measured. The benefit is the hoped-for achievement of an agreed objective. This objective is measured, maybe in monetary terms if profit is expected, maybe in terms of some non-monetary factor which the company is seeking to change, for example, the number of rejects.

Thirdly, responsibility for achieving the objective, and a willing committment to it, is taken on by someone who has the power in the organization to achieve it.

Fourthly, accountancy techniques are used, but in a secondary role, to estimate detailed costs of the whole project (all components of the plan, not just IT), and to show what the financial effects will be if business expectations are achieved. Various levels of achievement may well be tested. Accountancy techniques are, of course, also used to monitor achievement.

The main weakness of the approach is that it treats each IT investment as a contributor to a separate and identifiable goal. Much of the IT spend is on infrastructures however, which cannot be justified by specific objectives.

4 Necessity

The most realistic approach, and one which copes with the need to lay down IT infrastructures, recognizes that IT systems are a necessity.

No attempt is made to measure the benefit in monetary terms. Objectives are agreed at board level however, and measured. These objectives consist of levels of performance needed to make some essential contribution to production, distribution or marketing strategy, to employee fulfillment, or to corporate survival. IT is managed on the basis of cost control, and the achievement of the performance objectives.

Case

The IT director of a large international bank is speaking: 'I'm sick and tired of hearing how easy it is for the banks and the airlines. How IT is in the front line of our businesses. How we don't have any problems with value for money. Take the automatic tellers. The high street cash dispensers we put in, at a cost that runs out of noughts on my calculator. They're called "hole in the wall" technology. Well, they're well-named. We can't point to any material benefits in the bank. All the value goes straight through the wall to the customer. The whole investment falls into the category of "IT is a competitive necessity".'

66 These capture market share examples are special cases. They are irrelevant to the bulk of IT spend. They should be taken out of the argument 99

66 Study after study shows that there is no simple correlation between IT spend and business success 99

66 IT is never used on its own. It's value is its effect on the business factor you're seeking to excel in 99

30% OF COMPANIES NOW JUSTIFY IT INVESTMENT BY THE ACHIEVEMENT OF NECESSARY PERFORMANCE OBJECTIVES RATHER THAN FINANCIAL BENEFITS.

Section 4
What they Say

❝ Throughout the whole journey, you have a vision, and a hope. Only when you arrive can you say 'It's fantastic,' or 'My God, we should never have come ❞

❝ Very often users ask for the system, and leave it to the IT director to force out the benefits. But if you sponsor it, you're responsible for benefits. Our job is to audit that they've been delivered ❞

❝ It's rare for boards to say no to technology projects. The main benefits are intangible. They say 'But we've got no option, have we?' ❞

❝ Value is milestones. If IT strategy is vital to achieving those milestones, that is value ❞

❝ Most of what individuals spend doesn't result in a financial benefit. It is intended to bring fulfilment, and to ensure the future. When we do spend to reap profit, what do we use the profit for? More fulfilment, and to better ensure the future. Why shouldn't businesses and governments behave like individuals? ❞

❝ Quality of life is the issue. The effort you put in at work in the '80s is not acceptable in the '90s. This means more people, unless you support them with IT. Families and life style are more important, work is becoming equated with social life. People handle their domestic affairs from work. A certain level of IT is becoming a basic part of acceptable working conditions ❞

❝ Why do we seek to justify the inevitable? We must have information. In a company of any size, paper systems have failed us. You can't make information of any quality available without electronic means. If it is essential that we spend, we don't have to identify the benefits. All we have to do is to control the cost ❞

66 It's no good following lemmings over the cliff. Having said that, you have to look at your spend in relation to your competitors. And if you find yourself saying 'That's twice ours!' can you hope to compete with them? 99

66 If you want to be a certain type of business, you've got to have a certain IT system 99

66 The telephone system here is a good analogy. We question what we spend. And we question its efficiency. But no one has ever asked what is it worth 99

66 At board level we say we are right, the users are wrong – because we're taking the helicopter view 99

66 Our IT is justified by business drivers. The ultimate business drivers. Not cost/benefit analyses but survival. Not just bankruptcy, but life and death 99

66 IT has become an issue at every turn 99

66 There are these two camps. Camp A says we're spending an awful lot of money, we must see bottom line for it. B says we take business investment decisions by putting our hands on our hearts and going for it. Why not IT? The reason for A is a distrust of IT 99

In a section on 'What they say', there is nothing this book can add.

Part 4

CONCLUSION

66 I would like to think that it was an educational problem. Unfortunately it's not that simple. Because we have no teachers. We are travelling in unexplored territory, and, since no one has been there before, it's very dangerous to listen to anyone who says he knows the way 99

Chapter 8

Power and Responsibility

"I don't know whether you think that management is a science. But if it is, then it will have its laws. And one of these laws is that you never separate power and responsibility. Never give someone the responsibility for doing something, if you haven't given them the power to achieve it. Even more important, never give anyone the power to do something, if they are not held responsible for the results. Now the introduction of computers to organizations was accompanied by the biggest travesty of this law since the industrial revolution started, in the eighteenth century. Because the users, bless their hearts, still had responsibility for achieving business results. But their power to achieve them was continually eroded, as they relied, more and more, on computer systems they had neither the time, nor the expertise, to control"

We are nearly at the end. Of a century. Of this book. And of a beginning: a clumsy, brave, naive and brash attempt to mechanize the brain, to automate wherever it was bound down by drudgery, lost for speed, baffled by complexity or simply bored obeying necessary rules.

One might argue that the end of a beginning is followed by the beginning of the end! What can we predict for the next century, what message is there from this book, what insight can we gain which provides a talisman to guide us to the end of a rather troubled childhood for the computer?

It's a nasty moment. We have done all our research. IT directors, everywhere, have told us what they think. We have, on our desk, a mass of cases and quotations. They have been carefully colour-coded; but all the highlighter pens are now back in their case.

It's been wonderful, eye-opening, a stimulating privilege. And now the crunch. What ails us doctor, and what is the cure?

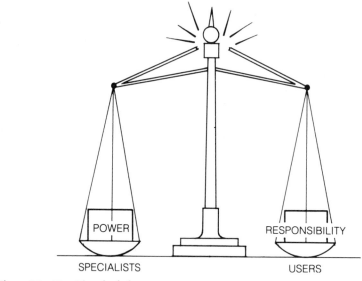

Figure 8.1 Upsetting the balance

Fortunately, it jumps off every page.

The problem is all-pervasive. Every difficulty, every bad-news story, every hard-to-justify investment – they all speak of it.

When we first brought a computer into the firm, we broke a rule. And we went on breaking it, most of us, right up to Watershed. Nothing naughty about it. It wasn't deliberate. No one knew then what the consequences would be. Even if they had, it's hard to see how it could have been otherwise.

Because the rule we broke was Never Separate Power and Responsibility. And, in those days, no one was going to give computer technicians responsibility for our businesses. Nor give computer users, mere laymen, the power to touch the switches.

Let's spell it out. We bought a new sort of machine. To automate somebody's work.

But they couldn't use it. It was too complicated. So we took on a manager to automate the work. We were careful, however, not to give him the responsibility for what the work was about.

And he was careful not to take it. That stayed right where it was. The users of the computer retained responsibility for business performance. But the systems they used to achieve this performance, imposed on them in many cases in the early days, and on which they eventually came to depend, were designed and run by the computer manager.

The quality of these systems, their responsiveness, accuracy, even the rules they followed much of the time, were in the hands of the analysts and programmers.

The organizational rupture this caused could not have been more plainly expressed than by the bank manager, in the late '60s, who was confronted by an angry customer, complaining that the statement of his account was inaccurate. He excused himself. 'I'm afraid that's the computer,' he said.

Was the customer to complain, then, to the computer manager, to the IT department, perhaps to the computer itself?

How can we hold anyone responsible for a result they no longer have the power to achieve? How can we expect benefits from an investment, if we leave it in the hands of someone not responsible for achieving these benefits?

'It happens,' you are saying. 'Look at the accounts department. Or the canteen. The accounts manager, the canteen manager; they each, in their way, have power over our figures. But we do not hold them responsible for business results.'

Ah, but we do. To the extent that their work impinges on business results. If the debtors are not chased, if the factory output falls due to food poisoning, these two managers will be held accountable.

The thing about computers is that their work impinges on every department's efforts to achieve business results. And not exceptionally, like a mistake in the accounts, or a culinary disaster. Practically every action, every decision, is affected by IT systems, and they are affected all the time, as a matter of routine.

Impinges is too weak a word. IT permeates the organization. Every manager's power to achieve results depends on the information systems.

But, if these systems are technology based, the likelihood is that they were designed by people who reported to an IT department, and who felt justified in taking matters into their own hands since they believed, and often said, that the users did not know what they wanted.

The symptoms of this division of power and responsibility are clear and suffered by all.

Criticism of the IT department, for example. A costly addition to the overheads. Where are the benefits from all the money we've poured in? Never met a deadline yet. The systems can't respond; they're slow, and don't really deliver what we want. Trouble is, they're not business oriented, none of them. Never had to run a business operation in their lives.

What is the culture gap but a symptom of not having to take responsibility? If IT people had responsibility for business results, can we doubt the alacrity with which they would have acquired the business nous they are said to lack? And once users are given responsibility for IT they make mistakes, sure – but they learn fast. The whole we/they atmosphere that used to bedevil IT, with 'lack of participation' slogans levelled at the users, who replied by injecting both venom, and pitying laughter, in their opinions of the analysts and programmers they branded as 'techies' – it's still there in many cases, an enduring monument to separatism.

What was the swing to decentralization, and the go-it-alone user trend, but a reaction to loss of power from people who were being held accountable for results?

What is the programming backlog, but a demand for a service from departments who do not have the problems of providing it? If they had to write the programs, they'd soon stop asking for them.

This is the picture of our industry. Exciting, in the van of progress, leading the information revolution. But it has its failings. It suffers, in a word, from separatism.

Restoring the balance, marrying power and responsibility, is key to the role of IT directors.

Recall, for a moment, the argument. Why should we have an IT director? There was the 'we've got problems' argument. Runaway spend, users taking IT matters into their own hands, and can IT give us competitive edge, or are we being led by the technology? Let's appoint someone we can trust to sort it all out.

If this someone's any good, however, he's going to succeed. And when he's sorted it all out, he can go back to what he was doing before. This argument supposes the appointment is temporary therefore.

What is the argument for a permanent director of information technology? There were only two reasons. Either IT becomes a line department, up there with marketing and production, dealing with the customer, influencing revenue and in the front line of the business.

Or the function deserves board representation because it is so important. Like our accountant, or company secretary, we need someone sage to advise us, and protect us, on IT matters, if good or bad performance in this area is fundamental to corporate survival.

During our discussions on these two arguments, earlier in the book, we saw that there was really no substance in either of them. The whole line and staff argument, what is in the front line and what is support, what is the business, and what is merely secondary, depends on what is critical to business success at a particular time. In the last analysis, the line and staff argument is exactly the same as the importance argument. Is IT that important? We're back to the banks and airlines syndrome. In some industries, at certain times, and under certain managements, it is. Or, should we say, it is perceived to be so. In others, it's not.

Restoring the balance of power and responsibility is what is key to the role of IT directors. There is no argument based on the importance of the subject. Or on the line rather than support thesis. It's all about responsibility. If you're responsible for business results you're important, and you're in line.

It is the only prescription for survival. By the year 2000, the only directors with the title IT, or, irrespective of title, having corporate responsibility for IT, will be those who have identified a computer-based improvement or survival strategy, and placed their heads on the block.

> THE ONLY PASSPORT TO CONTINUED REPRESENTATION ON THE BOARD IS TO ACCEPT RESPONSIBILITY FOR THE ACHIEVEMENT OF SIGNIFICANT BUSINESS RESULTS.

Any other claim is tenuous or temporary.

The text so far has been littered with quotations. Our intention was to rest from them in this last chapter, and to reflect more on their collective message. But there is one so pertinent, and so heartfelt, that we beg an exception. An IT director gave his opinion on the way to the board. Whether it was said in criticism of IT wizards, or of boards who do not give them recognition, doesn't really matter. It works in either case. He said:

'You don't get far as a technocrat intruding into the business.'

What are the solutions? Well, if power has been given to the technocrats, while responsibility continues to rest with the users, there are only two ways we can restore the balance. We can give IT power to the users or give business responsibility to the IT department.

Or, to put it another way, there are only two ways the IT director can assume responsibility for business results. He can, himself, become a user, or the IT department can move into the front line.

It's not all gloom and doom. Some have already done these things. Others are well on the way.

Case

A major clearing bank gave the IT director the responsibility for running its branches, which were dominated by the IT systems he'd installed.

Case

A large food chain, operating in the US and Europe, decentralized all its IT applications, giving the power to design and implement them to the users. The IT director, however, was given responsibility for designing a core system, which would ensure these separately implemented applications were integrated. He was then given responsibility for improving business performance through a policy of increased vertical integration. Part of his strategy depended on extending the degree of IT integration, the corporate database, electronic mail and EDI systems driven by the centralized core systems.

A recapitulation. The four main problems facing IT directors, each meriting a separate chapter, are the culture gap, managing the right degree of IT decentralization, managing the development of IT systems, and getting value for IT money.

A clue. Some claim that a happy marriage between power and responsibility is, on its own, an elixir sufficient to cure all these ills.

Case

The IT director of a US financial institution had resisted the pressures for wholesale decentralization, and started building a core system in the early '80s, as soon as the technology made the idea feasible. He claimed that the strategy had, over the last ten years, gradually cured the problems which were troubling most other installations. 'The simplest formula for correcting the power responsibility gap,' he said, 'is the splitting of IT systems into applications and infrastructures, and then decentralizing the applications. Magically, the programming backlog goes and value for money appears – the users automate what they can afford. The culture gap closes when the users do their own thing, and a correct balance of centralization and decentralization is achieved. What is common is centralized. And what is centralized determines survival. Which is the reason for my appointment. The company wants an IT director's salary where his mouth is.'

In the first chapter, we said four important and disturbing insights had been gained as a result of the research carried out. It may seen a bit late in the book to reveal what they are. But they have already appeared many times. What follows is only a summary.

The first is that a number of established management techniques don't work when applied to computers. We saw that the organization technique of identifying line and staff functions, a technique of respectable antiquity expounded in early Roman military treatises and before, shows some weaknesses when attempting to fit IT into an organization. We saw that established project management techniques of work measurement and particularly, of adding more resources, don't yield the expected results. We saw that investment techniques which, reasonably enough, attempt to measure benefits, do not provide management with sufficient decision making capability.

The second, and perhaps most disturbing, is that a number of IT directors believe that automation has put their organizations in a potentially out-of-control situation. However scare-mongering and sensational the statement appears, it is backed up by analytical and sensible argument – we no longer understand our programs, we cannot alter them beyond quite small limits, we are wide open to system penetration, and the complexity of the control systems we have built continues to increase exponentially as we add more and more. The crunch is, we totally depend on these systems.

Thirdly, the research shows that, so far from being able to delegate IT responsibility for what seems to be a specialized area, the chief executive has a key role in its successful use. He has a job to do that no one else can do. IT affects every department, every function and every manager in the business. And not always pleasantly. It attacks autonomy. The use of IT continually raises issues where the good of the company has to be argued against the good of a particular department. People have to change their ways. Insistence is sometimes required. Only the chief can fulfil this role.

Finally, we discovered hidden agendas. In such quantity that they turned what, in other areas, is normally an innocent and unimportant subterfuge, into an apparently necessary management technique. Nearly all IT directors are playing a double game. They have no choice. While education fails to close the culture gap, and boards insist on measured value for money, the only way to lead the company into an exploitable, or at least, defensible position in the information revolution, is to take it there in a series of disguised but palatable steps. 'Look, here are the savings!' we say. Only later can we point out 'Look, we survived!'

We must regret the hidden agenda. We must regret its necessity. But, until the culture gap is closed, IT directors must work at curing it in the ways they have found most successful. It is a lonely life however. And it has a dangerous element of 'We know best' about it. The strength of the board must eventually lie in its collective perception of what to do.

Since this book is based entirely on the opinions of others, it is fitting that we end with yet another quotation, from yet another IT director.

We thanked him for giving so much of his time to our research, and said: 'What would you most like to see in the book?

He replied:

'My hope would be that other directors, not just IT, and particularly the chief executive, are persuaded to read the message. Somehow you've got to get across to them the critical nature of total board involvement in the strategic planning of IT. If they don't do that, both IT and the organization are lost.'

Index